Making Holiday Folk Toys & Figures

Sharon Pierce

Sterling Publishing Co., Inc.   New York

Other Books by Sharon Pierce
Making Folk Toys & Weather Vanes
Making Whirligigs & Other Wind Toys
Making Old-Time Folk Toys

Edited by Michael Cea
Photography by Mark Atkinson

Library of Congress Cataloging-in-Publication Data

Pierce, Sharon.
  Making holiday folk toys & figures.

  Includes index.
  1. Wooden toy making.   2. Folk art—United States.
3. Holiday decorations.   4. Making holiday folk toys and
figures.   I. Title.
TT174.5.W6P544 1987   745.592   87–15141
ISBN 0-8069-6604-1 (pbk.)

Copyright © 1987 by Sharon Pierce
Published by Sterling Publishing Co., Inc.
Two Park Avenue, New York, N.Y. 10016
Distributed in Canada by Oak Tree Press Ltd.
c/o Canadian Manda Group, P.O. Box 920, Station U
Toronto, Ontario, Canada M8Z 5P9
Distributed in the United Kingdom by Blandford Press
Link House, West Street, Poole, Dorset BH15 1LL, England
Distributed in Australia by Capricorn Ltd.
P.O. Box 665, Lane Cove, NSW 2066
Manufactured in the United States of America
All rights reserved

TABLE OF CONTENTS

For my husband, Ryan, with love

A special thank-you to my children Ryan, Randy, Christopher, Kristin, and Kira for their continuing patience and enthusiasm; to Mark Atkinson for proceeding to shoot photographs during a snowstorm; and to everyone at Sterling involved in publishing this book, particularly Michael Cea, the editor.

EDITOR'S NOTE

Patterns for some of the toys are too large to reproduce in this book. They have been reduced, therefore, by 25% and printed on top of a ¾-in. grid. To enlarge these patterns so that you can use the sizes of materials given in the directions, buy 1-in. grid paper or make your own. Draw a portion of the original pattern one square at a time. Make the line running through the 1-in. square correspond directly to the line running through the book's ¾-in. square. After enlarging the pattern in this way, cut it out and continue instructions for making the posterboard pattern.

METRIC EQUIVALENCY CHART

MM—MILLIMETRES   CM—CENTIMETRES

INCHES TO MILLIMETRES AND CENTIMETRES

INCHES	MM	CM	INCHES	CM	INCHES	CM
⅛	3	0.3	9	22.9	30	76.2
¼	6	0.6	10	25.4	31	78.7
⅜	10	1.0	11	27.9	32	81.3
½	13	1.3	12	30.5	33	83.8
⅝	16	1.6	13	33.0	34	86.4
¾	19	1.9	14	35.6	35	88.9
⅞	22	2.2	15	38.1	36	91.4
1	25	2.5	16	40.6	37	94.0
1¼	32	3.2	17	43.2	38	96.5
1½	38	3.8	18	45.7	39	99.1
1¾	44	4.4	19	48.3	40	101.6
2	51	5.1	20	50.8	41	104.1
2½	64	6.4	21	53.3	42	106.7
3	76	7.6	22	55.9	43	109.2
3½	89	8.9	23	58.4	44	111.8
4	102	10.2	24	61.0	45	114.3
4½	114	11.4	25	63.5	46	116.8
5	127	12.7	26	66.0	47	119.4
6	152	15.2	27	68.6	48	121.9
7	178	17.8	28	71.1	49	124.5
8	203	20.3	29	73.7	50	127.0

PREFACE

As our country has become more automated and more computerized, the population, as a whole, has had more leisure time. Just consider the number of people flocking to movie theatres, golf courses, aerobic classes, and other recreational activities.

This book will enable you to devote some of your spare time to woodworking. Whether you are a beginning woodworker or a master craftsman, the projects will be just as satisfying.

Only basic tools and materials are needed to complete any of the folk figures or toys, and explicit, step-by-step directions are provided for each individual project. These folk figures and toys are perfect gifts to give during the various holiday seasons and on special occasions.

When selecting a project to make for a child, please remember that these toys are not suitable for small children who put everything into their mouths, unless the toys are kept on a shelf until the children are older.

Although the designs in this book are original, they are more simplistic than primitive. And like most folk art, these designs are figures of people, animals, and things common to all of us.

CONTEMPORARY FOLK ART

Folk Art. This is the term given to the art of the common man—one unschooled in artistic ways.

There has been great interest in American folk art since the early 1900s. Since that time, many museums across the country have developed collections that are exclusively of American folk art, such as the Abby Aldrich Rockefeller Folk Art Center, Williamsburg, Virginia and the Museum of American Folk Art, New York. Over the last few decades, the larger museums followed suit, and the majority now include folk art as part of their ongoing collection.

Although many pieces of early-American folk art date back from the early 1900s through to the late 1700s, interest in true folk art has not dwindled. Collectors and museums are always looking for excellent contemporary folk art. Sometimes it is a fine line that divides the artist and the folk artist, but a primitive, naive depiction is often worthy of a collector's investigation.

It may seem quite easy to make a "simple-looking" primitive piece, but the opposite is true, particularly if one has been "taught" artistic methods. However, for the self-taught carver or painter, this may be the only look he is able to obtain, and this is what folk art is all about.

In most respects, contemporary folk art does not differ from early-American folk art; many of the materials and tools used are still very similar. However, the original intent and purpose of the folk artists surely differ. Early settlers made what we often term today as folk art—carvings, toys, quilts, signs, and weather vanes—as utilitarian objects. Most folk art today appears to be made for decorative and collectible purposes. Even though the items may be used for what they were made for, they are not usually "necessities."

There exists in America today a sense of wanting to identify with our heritage and traditions. Ordinary people want to bring that sense of American heritage into the home, and one way to do this is through the creation of contemporary folk art.

Illus. 1. Statue of Liberty centerpiece.

DECORATING WITH FOLK ART

Whether you have a one-hundred-year-old weather vane or a new folk art figure, the same question arises: How should it be displayed in order to give it a special place in your home?

There are, of course, many variables here since individuals' homes and furnishings differ, but there are some basic guidelines to use for displaying.

If the piece you are working with is rather large, it is usually best to display it alone in a prominent location in a room. This does not necessarily mean right in the middle of the room, but possibly in a corner setting or on a wall where it will catch your eye as you enter the room.

Smaller items, such as the folk figures, are best displayed as a grouping. Mix projects of various heights.

Concentrating on a theme, such as rabbits and rabbit-related figures, will enable you to incorporate items made from different mediums, i.e., clay rabbits, wood rabbits, tin rabbits, etc. These can be grouped attractively on a shelf or on a tabletop.

Another display alternative is to arrange settings. For example, use wooden watermelon slices and the lamb eating watermelon or make an unusual centerpiece, such as the Statue of Liberty (Illus. 1). A centerpiece is a particularly effective way to feature your folk art on special occasions—Christmas, Halloween, Easter, or even a bridal shower.

However you decide to decorate with your old or new pieces of folk art, remember one thing—keep it simple!

GENERAL INSTRUCTIONS

The projects in this book are all relatively simple and the instructions given so explicit that even a beginner in woodworking will be able to make a successful folk art figure or toy.

Always read the instructions and check the materials list before beginning any project. If you have materials on hand that can be substituted, don't hesitate to use them.

Some of the figures and toys require various thicknesses of wood; unless you use the correct thickness, the project may appear out of proportion. Pine is the wood most often stated in the materials list, as it is readily obtainable and easy to work with; however, hardwoods can also be used.

Most patterns in this book are actual size, but any that are not are printed on top of a grid to enable you to enlarge them by hand. You can also enlarge them on many of the new copy machines.

Use transparent tracing paper to trace the patterns for the project from the book. Transfer each pattern onto poster board; once this pattern is cut out, you will be able to use it many times.

After the pattern is cut out, trace the outline onto wood. Make sure that you use the proper thickness of wood.

Cutting can be done with either a scroll saw or band saw. Be sure to use a ⅛-in. blade if you have to make any intricate or very curved cuts. Use extreme care not to injure yourself when cutting any small pieces, such as ears, arms, and legs. Use a scroll saw for any small pieces that have to be cut.

For projects requiring drilling, only a small, portable drill is needed. Always test-drill into scrap wood to check the accuracy of the bit you are using, especially if it will be used to hold a wooden dowel.

In most cases, sanding can be done entirely by hand. However, if you have a small, stationary sander, you can save time by using it for the majority of the sanding. For the first sanding, use a medium-grade sandpaper. Finishing or final sanding should be done by hand with a fine-grade sandpaper.

Detailed mixing instructions are given for the painting of each project. Since these measurements are approximate, slight adjustments may be needed in the amounts given. A list of the basic colors used throughout the book is given on page 16.

When gluing is required, always be sure

to allow time for the glue to set and dry thoroughly before handling the project again. Also give ample time for the paint and stain to dry before assembling the folk figures and toys.

Copper wire is used to fasten arms and legs in many of the projects. Any medium-to-stiff 14 gauge wire can be used. If the toy is meant to move freely, do not tighten the wires against the arms and legs, unless positioning is desired.

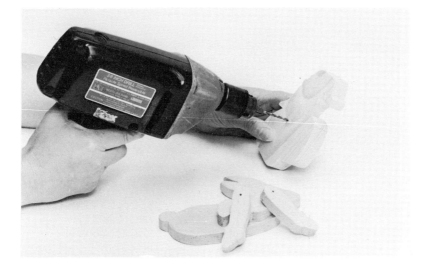

Illus. 2. Drilling.

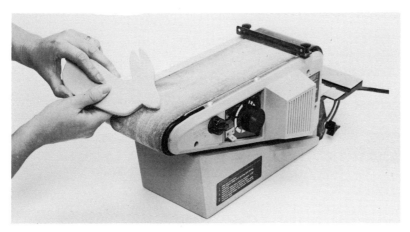

Illus. 3. Sanding.

MATERIALS & EQUIPMENT

Following is a brief summary and description of the materials and equipment you will need to make the folk figures and toys in this book.

Materials

WOOD

The majority of projects require ¾- or ⅜-in. pine. Some figures or toys require ¼-in. birch plywood, a premium-grade plywood. Other woods, such as hardwoods, may be substituted, but the thicknesses should remain the same. Always choose a good-quality wood, as this is the basic material for all projects.

WOODEN DOWELS

Various-size dowels are used for several of the toys. Since the diameter of a dowel varies from one to another, always test-drill in scrap wood to check for proper fit and correct bit selection.

WOODEN FINIALS

Wooden finials are pieces of wood that have been turned on a lathe. They are used for the jester acrobat toy (page 120), and are available from hardware dealers.

DRAWER PULLS

Manufactured in assorted sizes, these wooden balls are used decoratively for the monkey acrobat (page 119) and as a counterbalancing weight for the jumping jockey (page 123).

¼"

⅜"

¾"

Illus. 4. Thicknesses of wood.

COPPER WIRE

Copper wire is available in various gauges at hardware dealers'. Fourteen-gauge is the thickness used to attach arms and legs of folk figures in order to have moveable joints. Bend the copper wire with needle-nose pliers.

METAL WIRE

Choose a stiff 1/16-in.-diameter wire for the jumping jockey (page 123). The wire should be bendable, but stiff enough to hold its form with a weight on one end. Use 16-gauge, bendable wire for the camels (page 84).

JUTE TWINE

Jute twine is thin, rope-like twine that is used in several projects, such as the camels and the donkey (page 72).

FELT

Felt is medium-weight fabric that is made of fibres that are pressed together and steamed. Use black felt for the standing Santa's bag (page 60).

WOOLLY FABRIC

Sometimes referred to as sherpa, woolly fabric is often used as lining in a heavy coat. This fabric is used for the lamb with the watermelon (page 36).

BRASS BELLS

Bells come in assorted sizes and shapes, but the bells required for the camels in the Nativity scene (page 77) are 1/2-in. brass jingle bells.

SANDPAPER

Most sanding, whether done by hand or machine, requires medium-grade paper. Final sanding should always be done by hand with a fine-grade sandpaper.

PAINT

Most of the figures and toys require the application of acrylic tube paints. The basic colors that are used repeatedly on the projects are:

Illus. 5. Painting a folk art figure.

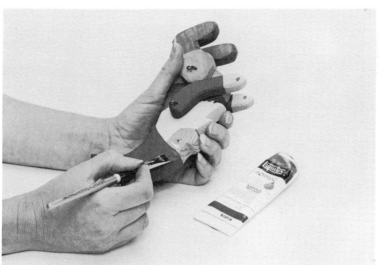

titanium white
burnt umber
turner's yellow
naphthol red light
red oxide
cerulean blue hue
permanent green deep
hooker's green
Since color is a matter of preference, other colors may be substituted.

STAIN
Several of the folk figures require stains instead of paint. There are many brands and colors available; choose a quality brand for best results.

BRUSHES
It is best to have several sizes of brushes. Choose artist-quality brushes in ¼-, ½-, ¾-, and 1-in. sizes.

WOOD GLUE
Yellow wood glue should be used for all projects requiring glue. Clamp or weight sections that have been glued for a strong, durable bond.

TRACING PAPER
This is a transparent paper that is used to trace the patterns from the book.

POSTER BOARD
Make pattern templates with this thin cardboard, which is also known as "oak tag."

Equipment

GOGGLES
Eye protection of some sort should always be worn when cutting, sanding, or drilling.

DUST MASK
Dust masks are highly recommended when sawing and sanding wood; they are essential when working with mahogany and pressure-treated lumber.

TABLETOP SCROLL SAW
A scroll saw has a vibrating blade, and it is especially useful for small, intricate work. Choose a fine-tooth blade. Some scroll saws have a sanding wheel, which can perform the limited sanding required for the projects.

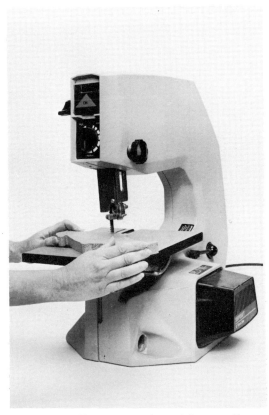

Illus. 6. Cutting with a scroll saw.

BAND SAW

A band saw has a thin, continuous blade. It is a versatile saw that can make intricate cuts or saw through a 4 x 4. Choose a ⅛-in. blade for intricate work and a ¼-in. blade for straight cuts.

SANDER

A small, stationary belt sander or sanding wheel on a scroll saw is adequate for the small amount of sanding required of each project. Use medium-grade sandpaper.

DRILL

Any portable hand drill is suitable; however, several different sizes of drill bits are essential.

NEEDLE-NOSE PLIERS

These thin, tapered pliers can bend and cut the copper wire used for the majority of figures and toys.

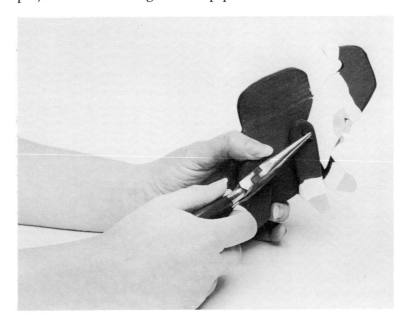

Illus. 7. Using needle-nose pliers to bend copper wire.

Folk Figures

American Indian

Reminiscent of the antique storefront Indians, this folk art Indian can be incorporated into a nice Thanksgiving centerpiece or used in a grouping with other folk figures.

MATERIALS

Pine, ¾ in. thick: 10 x 14 in.
Copper wire, 14 gauge: 5 in.
Acrylic paint: turner's yellow, naphthol red light, permanent green deep, red oxide, cerulean blue hue, mars black, titanium white, burnt umber
Stain: light-to-medium color
Wood glue
Sandpaper: medium and fine grades
Tracing paper
Poster board

TOOLS

Scroll saw or band saw
Stationary belt sander or sanding wheel
Drill with ³⁄₃₂-in. bit
Needle-nose pliers

INSTRUCTIONS

Pattern. Trace pattern pieces and transfer onto poster board. Cut out, and then trace patterns onto wood. Also trace on wood 2 square base pieces, one 3½ x 3½ in. and one 4½ x 4½ in.

Cutting. Using a scroll saw or band saw, cut out the Indian and base pieces. Be exceptionally careful while cutting out the Indian's feet.

Drilling. Drill a hole, using a ³⁄₃₂-in. bit,

Illus. 8.

through the arms and torso, as marked on the pattern (Illus. 9).

Sanding. Round all edges with the sander; then give each piece a final sanding, by hand, with a fine-grade sandpaper.

Illus. 9. Pattern for American Indian.

Gluing. Glue the small base piece to the large base piece. This should be perfectly centered. Next, glue the Indian's feet in place, making sure that he will stand properly. Set aside to dry.

Painting. Paint the Indian with the following paint mixtures. Remember that measurements are only approximate.
Base: 2 tsp. green / few drops black
Tunic, moccasins: 1½ tsp. red oxide
Pants: ½ tsp. yellow / ⅛ tsp. burnt umber
Hair, eyes: ¼ tsp. black
Belt, armbands, feather: ½ tsp. green / few drops black
Beads, buckle: ⅛ tsp. black / ⅛ tsp. white
Feathers: 1—⅛ tsp. green / ⅛ tsp. white
2—⅛ tsp. yellow

3—⅛ tsp. red
4—⅛ tsp. green
5—⅛ tsp. blue

Staining. When paint has dried completely, apply a light coat of stain over the entire Indian, including arms. (Do not stain the bottom of the feet.) Wipe off any excess and allow to dry.

Assembling. Cut a piece of copper wire to a length of 5 in. Insert one end into the bent arm. Using needle-nose pliers, bend the end in the crook of the arm into a small, closed loop. Slide the wire through the torso and the other arm. Bend this end of the wire into another closed loop.

Glue the Indian to the top of the base.

Illus. 10. Inserting end of wire into bent arm.

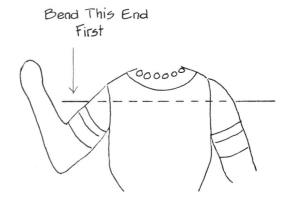

Statue of Liberty

Patriotic pieces are, by far, one of the most popular choices of folk artists both past and present. Make this symbol of freedom to pass on as an heirloom.

MATERIALS

Pine, ¾ in. thick: 10 x 20 in.
Pine, ⅜ in. thick: 3 x 4 in.
Birch plywood, ¼ in. thick: 6 x 6 in.
Wood, 2 x 4: 3½ in. long
Wooden dowel, ³⁄₁₆-in. diameter: 2-in. piece
Wood glue
Finishing nails, 2½ in. long (8d finish): two
Wire nails, 18 x ⅝: two
Acrylic paint: turner's yellow, cerulean blue hue, titanium white
Stain: light color
Sandpaper: fine and medium grades
Tracing paper
Poster board

TOOLS

Scroll saw or band saw
Stationary belt sander or sanding wheel
Drill with ³⁄₁₆-, ³⁄₃₂-in. bits
Hammer
Woodcarving tool: ¼-in. flat chisel (optional)
Small C-clamp (G-cramp), if carving detail

INSTRUCTIONS

Pattern. Trace pattern pieces and transfer onto poster board. Cut out, and then trace patterns onto wood. Trace the body

Illus. 11.

and arms onto ¾-in. wood. Patterns for flame and circular flame-holder should be traced onto ⅜-in. wood. Trace the crown onto ¼-in. wood.

Cutting. Cut out all pieces using a scroll saw or band saw. Also cut 2 base pieces

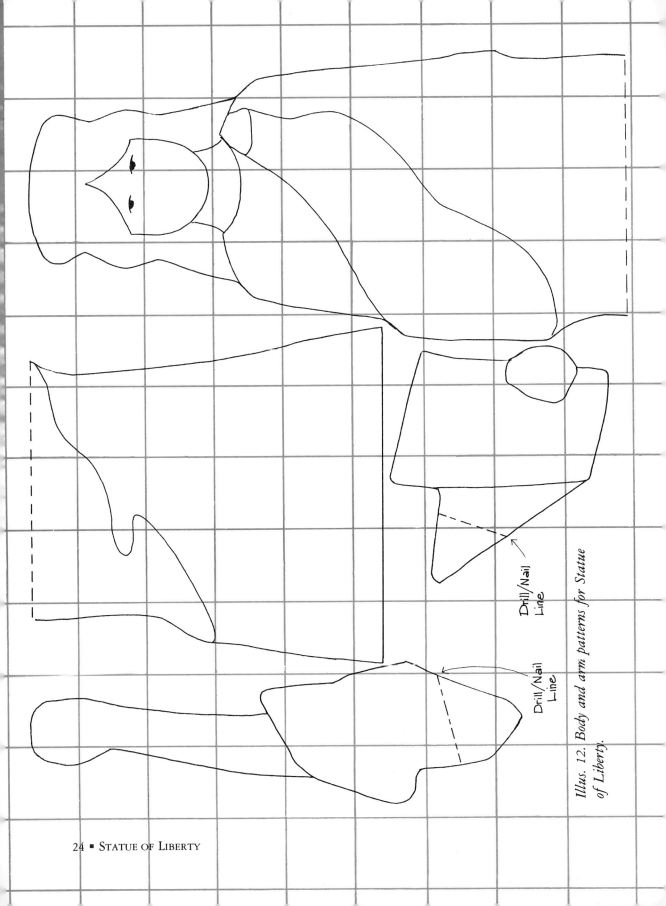

Illus. 12. Body and arm patterns for Statue of Liberty.

Drill/Nail Line

Drill/Nail Line

Illus. 13. Crown, flame, and flame holder patterns for Statue of Liberty.

from the ¾-in. wood: one 4½ x 4½ in., the other 5½ x 5½ in. Cut a 3½-in. length of 2 x 4 wood and a 2-in. length of ³⁄₁₆-in.-diameter dowel.

Also cut a small scrap ¾ x 2½ in. from ¾-in. wood; it will be used for a support piece to join the statue to the base.

Adjust the table of your saw to make a 30° angled cut. Cut off the back top section of the head (Illus. 14). This will enable the crown to sit at a proper angle.

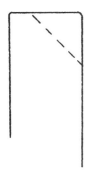

Illus. 14. Angle for cutting head.

Drilling. Using the ³⁄₁₆-in. bit, drill a hole through the hand to hold the torch. See Illus. 15 for correct angle. After you have drilled the hand, drill a corresponding hole into the circular torch base.

With the ³⁄₃₂-in. bit, drill a hole into each arm at the angle shown in Illus 12. Be

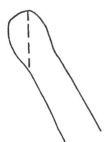

Illus. 15. Drilling angle for hand.

sure to use a bit slightly smaller than the diameter of the nail you will be using.

Carving. For a more dimensional look, carve details with a small carving chisel.

If you have never done any carving previously, practise on some scrap wood. Always clamp your workpiece down and keep your hands behind the blade at all times.

Carve detail by, first, pressing the chisel straight into the wood about ⅛ in. deep (Illus. 17). Do this in a continuous line. Go over all details again by placing the chisel ¹⁄₁₆ in. from the incised line (chisel should be held at a 45° angle, as shown in Illus. 18), and then pressing into the wood to meet the first cut. Continue around the design.

Sanding. Using the belt sander or sanding wheel, sand all edges until rounded. Give each piece a final sanding, by hand, with a fine-grade sandpaper. Carefully hand-sand carved details.

Gluing. Glue the arms in place, and then immediately hammer a nail into each previously drilled arm. The arm with the torch should extend forward slightly.

Also glue the base pieces together in ascending sizes. Finally, glue the torch together, and then set all pieces aside to dry.

Painting. This piece is painted to resemble the oxidized-copper color of the real Statue of Liberty. In order to achieve this, mix the approximate proportions given: 2 tsp. yellow / 1 tsp. blue / 1 tsp. white. Adjust as needed. The color will be softened when stain is rubbed over it.

Do not paint carved detail lines. If you have chosen not to carve, leave a ⅟₁₆-in. space unpainted where detail lines are in order to highlight these details.

Note: paint for face and arms should be watered down considerably. Also, paint ap- plied for the robe should be applied thickly to resemble draped fabric.

Assembling. First, take a small square of sandpaper and very lightly sand the painted pieces to give the statue an aged look.

Next, glue the crown in place; when dry, hammer finishing nails into the top of the crown.

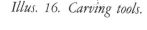

Illus. 16. Carving tools.

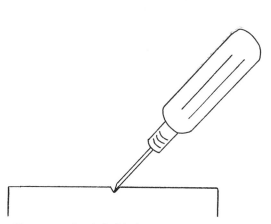

Illus. 17. Straight chisel cut.

Illus. 18. Angled chisel cut.

Position the torch in the hand, and then glue Lady Liberty diagonally across the base. Glue the support piece to the base and back of the statue (Illus. 19).

Stain the entire project, wiping off all excess immediately.

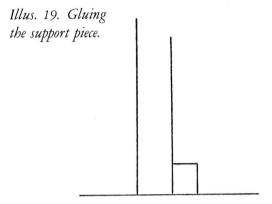

Illus. 19. Gluing the support piece.

Uncle Sam

Here's a perfect folk art figure to use as a centerpiece for picnics, especially the Fourth of July!

MATERIALS

Pine, ¾ in. thick: 8 x 13 in.
Birch plywood, ¼ in. thick: 3½ x 5 in.
Wood, 2 x 4: 4¼ in. long
Wooden dowel, ⅛ in. thick: 5 in. long
Copper wire, 14 gauge: 5¾ in. long
Acrylic paint: titanium white, naphthol red light, cerulean blue hue, mars black, burnt umber
Sandpaper: medium and fine grades
Wood glue
Tracing paper
Poster board

TOOLS

Scroll saw or band saw
Stationary belt sander or sanding wheel
Drill with ⅛- and ³⁄₃₂-in. drill bits and ⅛-in. extended drill bit
Needle-nose pliers

INSTRUCTIONS

Pattern. Trace pattern pieces and transfer onto poster board. Cut out poster-board patterns, and then trace Uncle Sam's body, arms, and shoes onto ¾-in. wood. Also draw a 4½ x 5½-in. base piece onto this thickness of wood. Trace the flag onto the ¼-in. wood.

Cutting. Cut out all the above pieces using a scroll saw or band saw. Then cut a 4¼-in. length of 2 x 4 wood. Also cut a

Illus. 20.

5-in. length of ⅛-in.-diameter wooden dowel.

Drilling. With the ³⁄₃₂-in. bit, drill a hole into the arms of Uncle Sam. Use the ⅛-in. bit to drill a hole into one of the hands. Drill this at a slight angle to the hand (Illus. 22).

Because the body is so wide, drill the hole through the width of the torso with the ⅛-in. extended drill bit. (If you have a good eye and can drill straight, you might be able to do the job using a regular ⅛- or ³⁄₃₂-in. bit, drilling in from both sides to meet in the center.)

Also drill a hole into the underside of the flag, as marked on the pattern (Illus. 21).

Illus. 21. Flag, arm, shoe, and body patterns for Uncle Sam.

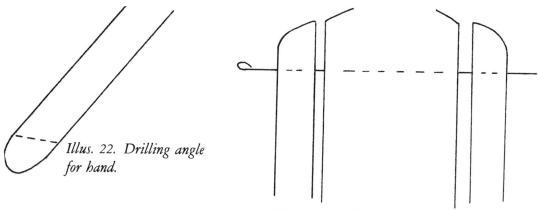

Illus. 22. Drilling angle for hand.

Illus. 23. Drilling lines.

Sanding. Use either a stationary belt sander or a sanding wheel to round the edges of each piece. Give each piece a final sanding, by hand, with a fine-grade paper.

Note: If carving of detail is desired, see page 26 for further instructions.

Painting. Paint Uncle Sam with the following paint mixtures. Measurements are only approximate.
Beard, stripes, base bottom: 2 tsp. white / few drops burnt umber
Vest, red stripes: 2 tsp. red / few drops black
Jacket, top base, trim, flag: 2 tsp.

blue / ⅛ tsp. white / ⅛ tsp. black
Shoes: ⅛ tsp. black
Face, hands: ⅛ tsp. white / drop red / drop burnt umber
Face detail: may be carved or painted.

Assembling. Cut a 5¾-in. length of copper wire. Using needle-nose pliers, bend one end into a small, closed loop. Attach the arms to the body, and then bend the other end of the wire into another loop.

Glue the base pieces together, and then glue the shoes to Uncle Sam. When dry, glue the figure to the base.

Glue the dowel into the flag and slide the dowel into Uncle Sam's hand.

Bride & Groom

This charming couple can be made to grace the table for a bridal shower or be given as a special remembrance of one's wedding. The hair, flowers, and groom's suit can be painted to match the individual couple.

MATERIALS

Pine, ¾ in. thick: 8 x 12 in.
Pine, ⅜ in. thick: 3 x 3 in.
Wooden dowel, ⅛ in. diameter: 3 in.
Acrylic paint: titanium white, mars black, burnt umber, naphthol red light, hooker's green
Stain: light color
Wood glue
Sandpaper: medium and fine grades
Tracing paper
Poster board

TOOLS

Scroll saw or band saw
Stationary belt sander or sanding wheel
Drill with ⅛-in. bit

INSTRUCTIONS

Pattern. Trace pattern pieces and transfer onto poster board. Cut out patterns and trace bride and groom bodies onto ¾-in. wood. Trace one arm from each pattern onto ⅜-in. wood.

Cutting. Using a scroll saw or band saw, cut out above pieces. Then, from ¾-in. wood, cut a 2½ x 5½-in. base piece and a 3½ x 6½-in. base piece.

Illus. 24.

Cut two 1-in. pieces of the ⅛-in.-diameter dowel.

Drilling. With a ⅛-in. bit, drill a hole into the outside shoulder of both the bride and the groom (Illus. 26). Drill a hole through the shoulder of each arm.

Sanding. Using a stationary belt sander or sanding wheel, round the edges of all pieces. Give each piece a final sanding, by hand, with a fine-grade paper.

Painting. Paint the bride and groom with the following paint mixtures. Remember that measurements are approximate.
Bride's gown, veil: 1 tsp. white / drop umber

Illus. 25. Patterns for bride and groom.

Groom's shirt: 1 tsp. white / drop umber

Vest, grey stripes: ½ tsp. white / ½ tsp. black

Jacket, black stripes, large base piece: 2 tsp. black

Hair, moustache: ½ tsp. red / ½ tsp. burnt umber

Face, hands, small base: watered-down burnt umber

Flowers: ¼ tsp. red / few drops white

Stems: ⅛ tsp. green

Assembling. Glue the base pieces together, and then glue the bride and groom together. (Bride should stand forward about ⅛ in. farther than the groom.) Glue the couple to the base.

Press a dowel piece into each arm and press into the corresponding shoulder. Dowels should protrude slightly.

If you wish to record the event, print the names and date on the front of the top base piece (Illus. 27).

Illus. 26. Back view of drilling and painting lines.

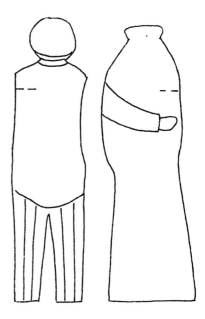

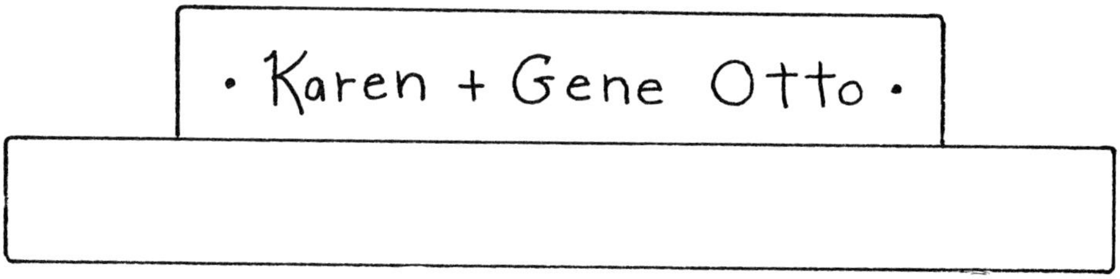

Illus. 27. Position of names on base.

Folk Animals

Lamb with Watermelon

Mary had a little lamb, and so can you!
This woolly lamb is fully jointed,
and he holds his own slice of watermelon.

MATERIALS
Pine, ¾ in. thick: 4 x 7 in.
Pine, ⅜ in. thick: 6 x 6 in.
White woolly material: 10 x 12-in. piece
Black felt: 2 x 2-in. piece
Copper wire, 14 gauge: 6 in.
Acrylic paint: mars black, titanium white,
permanent green deep, naphthol red light
White thread and needle
White glue
Sandpaper: medium and fine grades
Tracing paper
Poster board

TOOLS
Scroll saw or band saw
Stationary belt sander or sanding wheel
Drill with ³⁄₃₂-in. bit
Needle-nose pliers
Scissors

INSTRUCTIONS

Pattern. Trace pattern pieces and transfer
onto poster board. Cut out poster-board
patterns and trace body onto the ¾-in.
wood. Trace the legs and watermelon slice
onto ⅜-in. wood.

Lay the pattern for the "sheepskin" onto
the underside of the fabric; then pin and
cut around the pattern.

Trace 2 ears onto the black felt, using a

Illus. 28.

ball-point pen. Cut these out and set
aside.

Cutting. With a scroll saw or band saw,
cut out the body pieces for the lamb and
the piece for the watermelon slice.

Drilling. Drill a small hole into the
arms, legs, and body of the lamb using
the ³⁄₃₂-in. bit.

Sanding. Use the sander to sand all edges
of each piece. Create a carved look by
rounding the edges very well. Give each

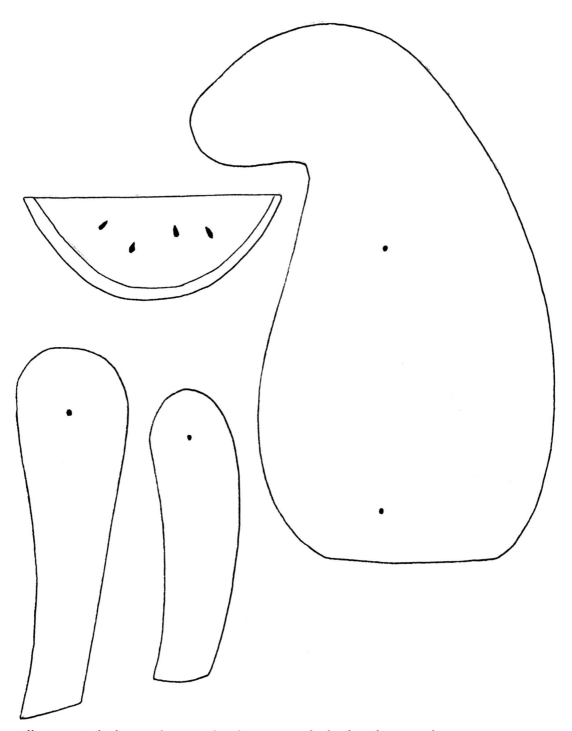

Illus. 29. Body, legs, and watermelon-slice patterns for lamb with watermelon.

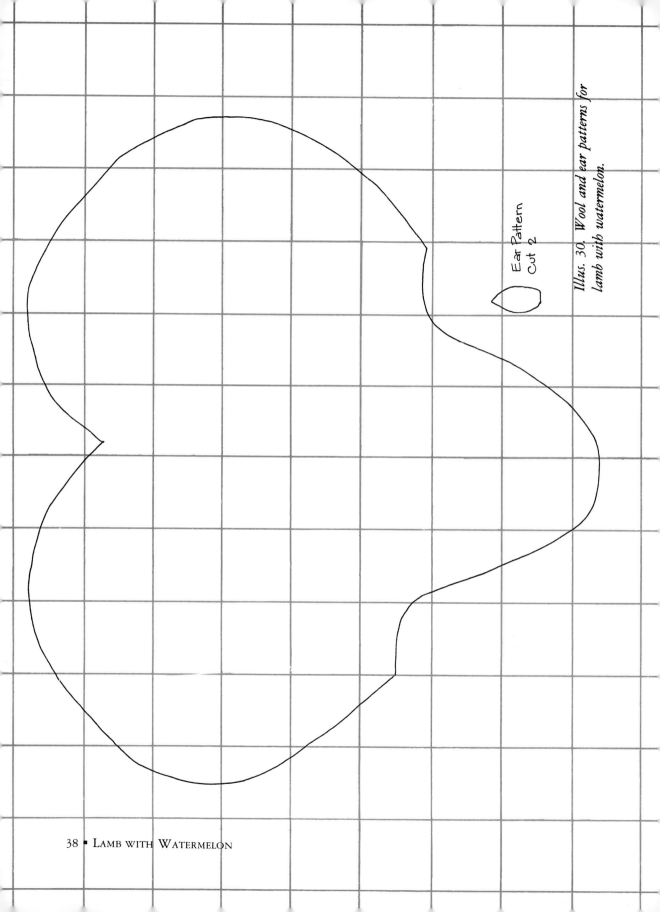

Ear Pattern
Cut 2

Illus. 30. Wool and ear patterns for lamb with watermelon.

piece a final sanding, by hand, with a fine-grade paper.

Painting. Paint the head, arms, and legs black. This requires only about one tsp. of paint. When dry, paint a small dot of white for the eye. Paint a smaller dot of black on top of the white dot to finish the eye.

Paint the main area of the watermelon with red (mix in a drop of black for a darker red). Paint the rind green, and then paint a few black seeds.

Assembling. Cut two 3-in. pieces of copper wire and bend one end of each into a small, closed loop (Illus. 31). Set these aside.

Illus. 31. Wire bent into a loop.

Wrap the lamb's wool around his body, as shown in Illus. 32, making sure that the wool fits snugly under the chin. There will be a gap around the face, but this will be adjusted with stitching.

When the body is positioned properly, hold the wool on both sides, and then poke a small hole into the wool at each corresponding spot where the holes are drilled in the wooden body.

While continuing to hold the body, insert a wire through one of the large legs, and then push it through the wool-covered body. Slide the other leg on the wire, and then bend this end of wire into a small, closed loop. Repeat with the remaining set of legs.

Overlap the wool where it meets along the stomach line and stitch together using a small overcast stitch. Take a small tuck on either side of the lamb's face, as shown in Illus. 33. Stitch securely.

Illus. 32. Sewing the lamb's wool around his body.

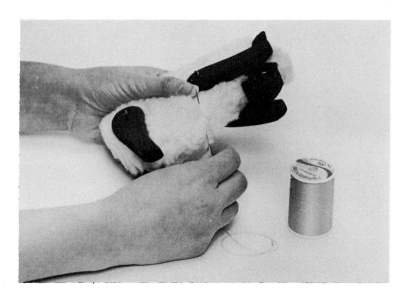

Now, glue the lamb ears in place using a small drop of glue. Tighten the copper wires so that the lamb will sit. Your lamb is now ready for his watermelon. Move the arms upwards to hold the melon slice securely.

Illus. 33. Stitching wool around lamb's face.

Sitting Reindeer

This jointed reindeer is a perfect example of whimsical folk art. Here he sits holding his own Christmas tree.

MATERIALS

Pine, ¾ in. thick: 3 x 5 in.
Pine, ⅜ in thick: 3 x 4 in.
Birch plywood, ¼ in. thick: 4 x 4 in.
Copper wire, 14 gauge: 6 in.
Small scrap of acrylic fur for tail (any kind)
Red ribbon, ⅛ in. wide: 12 in.
Acrylic paint: permanent green deep, naphthol red light, titanium white, mars black
Stain: medium color
Wood glue
Sandpaper: medium and fine grades
Tracing paper
Poster board

TOOLS

Scroll saw or band saw
Drill with 3⁄32-in. bit
Stationary belt sander or sanding wheel
Needle-nose pliers

INSTRUCTIONS

Pattern. Trace pattern pieces and transfer onto poster board. Cut out poster-board patterns, and then trace pattern for reindeer body onto ¾-in. wood. Trace the leg patterns onto ⅜-in. wood, and the ear, antler, and tree patterns onto ¼-in. wood.

Cutting. Using a scroll saw or band saw, cut out the reindeer body and legs. A ta-

Illus. 34.

bletop scroll saw should be used to cut out the remaining small pieces. Use extreme caution; the smaller the piece, the harder it is to hold while cutting.

To form the nose of the reindeer, make a ¼-in. cut into the nose from each side at the point where the nose joins the head. Make an additional cut from the front of the nose to meet both ¼-in. cuts, and the side sections of the nose will drop away, leaving only the center section.

Drilling. Drill holes, as indicated in Illus. 35, into the body and each leg, using the 3⁄32-in. bit.

Illus. 35. Patterns for sitting reindeer.

Sanding. Sand the body and the legs with the sander, rounding all edges. Sand the antlers, ears, and tree by hand, using a fine-grade paper. Also give a final hand-sanding to the body and legs.

Staining. Using a soft cloth, apply stain to all reindeer parts. Wipe off any excess stain and set pieces aside to dry.

Painting. Paint the tree with permanent green deep. This requires only about ¼ tsp. of paint.

Paint the nose of the reindeer red, and then paint a dot of white for the eye. When dry, paint a smaller black dot inside the white dot.

Assembling. Glue the reindeer's ears in place and set aside to dry; then glue the antlers in place, flat against the inside of the ears. Also glue the tree to one of the reindeer's hoofs.

Attach the legs by, first, cutting two 2¾-in. pieces of copper wire. Then, using needle-nose pliers, make a closed loop at one end of each wire. Position bottom legs on either side of the reindeer body. Insert a wire through the legs and body, and then loop the other end of the wire, tightening it against the reindeer. Legs should be moveable, but should still enable good positioning. Repeat this procedure with the top legs.

Tie a ribbon around the reindeer's neck, placing the bow in the back. Now, glue a small, approximately ½-in. square, piece of fur in place for the tail.

"Sky-High" Animals

This cow-goat-duck trio was inspired by the story about the Brementown Musicians. Make this piece of folk art for your favorite animal lover.

MATERIALS

Pine, ¾ in. thick: 8 x 10 in.
Pine, ⅜ in. thick: 5 x 7 in.
Birch plywood, ¼ in thick: 3 x 3 in.
Wooden dowel, ⅛-in. diameter: 1 in. long
Wood glue
Acrylic paint: titanium white, mars black, turner's yellow, burnt umber, naphthol red light, hooker's green
Sandpaper: medium and fine grades
Tracing paper
Poster board

TOOLS

Scroll saw or band saw
Stationary belt sander or sanding wheel
Drill with ⅛-in. bit

INSTRUCTIONS

Pattern. Trace pattern pieces and transfer onto poster board. Cut out poster-board patterns, and then trace cow onto ¾-in. wood. Also draw a 3¼ x 7½-in. base piece on the ¾-in. wood.

On the ⅜-in. wood, trace the goat and duck. Trace horns and ears onto ¼-in. wood.

Cutting. Using either a scroll saw or band saw, cut out the above pieces, except

Illus. 36.

the ears and horns, which should only be cut out with a tabletop scroll saw.

Drilling. Drill a hole, approximately ½ in. in depth, into the top of the goat and the bottom of the duck (Illus. 38). The holes should be drilled as straight as possible.

Sanding. With either a stationary belt sander or sanding wheel, round edges of all pieces. Round edges for the horns and ears by hand. Give each piece a final sanding, by hand, with a fine-grade sandpaper.

Painting. Paint "sky-high" animals with the following paints. Measurements are approximate.

Illus. 37. Patterns for "sky-high" animals.

Illus. 38. Drilling lines for duck and goat.

Duck, cow white, beard, horns: 1½ tsp. white / few drops burnt umber

Goat: ¼ tsp. black / ¼ tsp. white

Ears, cow black: ½ tsp. black

Beak: ⅛ tsp. yellow / drop red / drop burnt umber

Base: 1 tsp. green

Eyes: dot of white / dot of black

Assembling. Glue ears and horns in place; then, glue the cow to the base and set aside to dry. Glue the goat on top of the cow and, when dry, glue the duck on top of the goat, inserting dowel for added strength.

Running Horses

The particular shape of these horses is an adaptation of an antique weather vane that originally included an Indian riding bareback.

Although many pieces of folk art look good displayed as a group, this trio is quite effective if displayed individually.

MATERIALS

Pine, ¾ in. thick: 4½ x 20 in. (Base)
Pine, ⅜ in. thick: 12 x 24 in.
Wooden dowel, ³⁄₁₆-in. diameter: 18 in.
Acrylic paint: titanium white, burnt umber, naphthol red light, raw umber
Stain: medium color
Sandpaper: medium and fine grades
Tracing paper
Poster board

TOOLS

Scroll saw or band saw
Stationary belt sander
Drill with ³⁄₁₆-in. bit

INSTRUCTIONS

Pattern. Trace pattern piece and transfer onto poster board. Cut out the poster-board pattern, and then trace 3 times onto ⅜-in. wood.

Cutting. Using a scroll saw or band saw, cut out the horses; also cut out a 4½ x 20-in. base from the ¾-in. wood. Cut 3 lengths from the wooden dowel: one 4¼ in., one 5 in, and one 5½ in.

Drilling. Using a ³⁄₁₆-in. bit, drill holes into the base approximately ½ in. in depth. Holes should be staggered on the base for positioning of horses similar to the positions shown in the photograph. Illus. 41 indicates these positions.

Illus. 39.

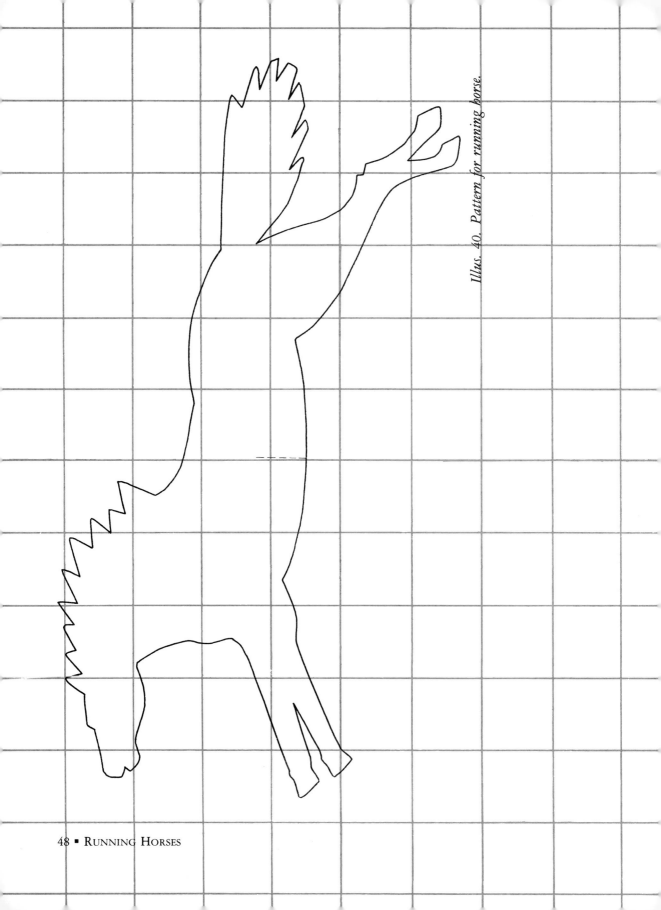

Illus. 40. Pattern for running horse.

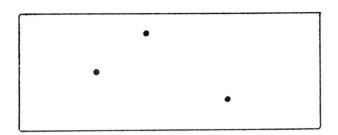

Also drill a hole into the underside of each horse, as indicated on the pattern (Illus. 40).

Sanding. Sand all edges of each piece using either a stationary belt sander or sanding wheel. Give each piece a final sanding, by hand, with a fine-grade sandpaper, paying special attention to the notches in the mane and tail.

Painting Paint the horses with the mixtures given below. Measurements are only approximate.
Manes, tails: 1½ tsp. white / few drops burnt umber

Horse 1: ½ tsp. burnt umber / ½ tsp. white
Horse 2: ½ tsp. burnt umber / ½ tsp. red
Horse 3: 1 tsp. raw umber

Staining. Stain the base with a medium color. This is best applied with a cloth. Wipe off any excess to avoid streaking.

Assembling. Insert the 4¼-in. dowel into horse 1, the 5-in. dowel into horse 3, and the 5½-in. dowel into horse 2. Press horses and dowels into place on the base with horse 1 front left, horse 2 back center, and horse 3 front right.

Folk Santas

Old-Fashioned Santa

This old-time Santa is quick and easy to make, and is certainly a nice addition to a folk art collection. Since many antique Santas had blue, gold, or green robes, you might choose one of these colors or make a series of Santas.

MATERIALS
Pine, ¾ in. thick: 5 x 10 in.
Pine, ⅜ in. thick: 2 x 3 in.
Wooden dowel, ⅛-in. diameter: 2 in. long
Copper wire, 14 gauge: 6 in.
Acrylic paint: titanium white, mars black, naphthol red light, permanent green deep
Wood glue
Sandpaper: medium and fine grades
Tracing paper
Poster board

TOOLS
Scroll saw or band saw
Stationary belt sander or sanding wheel
Drill with ⅛-, ³⁄₃₂-in. bits
Needle-nose pliers

INSTRUCTIONS

Pattern. Trace the pattern pieces and transfer onto poster board. Cut out the poster-board patterns, and then trace the tree onto the ⅜-in. wood. Trace remaining pieces onto the ¾-in. wood.

Cutting. Cut out all pieces with either a band saw or scroll saw. Also cut a 2-in. length of ⅛-in.-diameter dowel.

Illus. 42.

Drilling. Using a ³⁄₃₂-in. bit, drill a hole into the shoulder of each arm and through the torso; then drill a hole, using the ⅛-in. bit, into one of the hands. This hole should be drilled at a slight angle to hold the tree upwards.

Also drill a hole into the underside of the tree using the ⅛-in. bit.

Sanding. Round all edges well using either a stationary belt sander or sanding wheel. Give each piece a final sanding, by hand, with a fine-grade paper.

Illus. 43. Arm, Christmas tree, and body patterns for old-fashioned Santa.

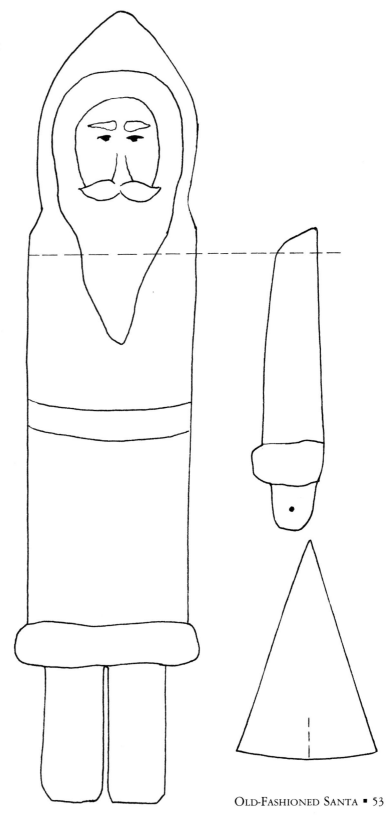

Painting. Paint Santa with the following colors. Measurements are approximate.
Robe: 1 tsp. red / few drops black
Beard, trim: ½ tsp. white
Belt, boots, base: ½ tsp. black
Tree, decorative trim: ½ tsp. green / drop black

Note: nose is pencilled in, eyes painted, and cheeks painted with a watered-down solution of red.

Assembling. Cut a 1¾-in. piece of copper wire and bend into a square using needle-nose pliers (Illus. 44); then cut a 3½-in. piece of copper wire and bend one end into a small, closed loop.

Illus. 44. Bending pattern for buckle.

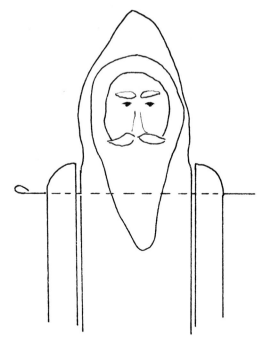

Illus. 45. Attaching arms with wire.

Attach the arms with the 3½-in. wire, (Illus. 45), and then bend the other end of the wire into a small loop. Tighten the wire against the arms to enable positioning.

Glue the dowel into the tree, and then place the tree in Santa's hand. Glue the belt buckle in place, and then glue Santa onto the base.

Santa on Reindeer

Santa's riding bareback, but he can also sit on the edge of the mantel. This delightful twosome can be made as a toy or used for a Christmas party centerpiece. If using them as a centerpiece, you can make a bed of holly or use greenery from your yard—add a few berries or oranges for extra color!

MATERIALS
Pine, ¾ in. thick: 11 x 12 in.
Pine, ⅜ in. thick: 4 x 5 in.
Birch plywood, ¼ in. thick: 2 x 3 in.
Copper wire, 14 gauge: 6 in.
Acrylic paint: permanent green deep, titanium white, burnt umber, naphthol red light, raw umber, mars black
Wood glue
Tracing paper
Poster board

TOOLS
Scroll saw or band saw
Stationary belt sander or sanding wheel
Drill with ³⁄₃₂-in. bit
Needle-nose pliers

INSTRUCTIONS

Pattern. Trace pattern pieces and transfer onto poster board. Cut out poster-board

Illus. 46.

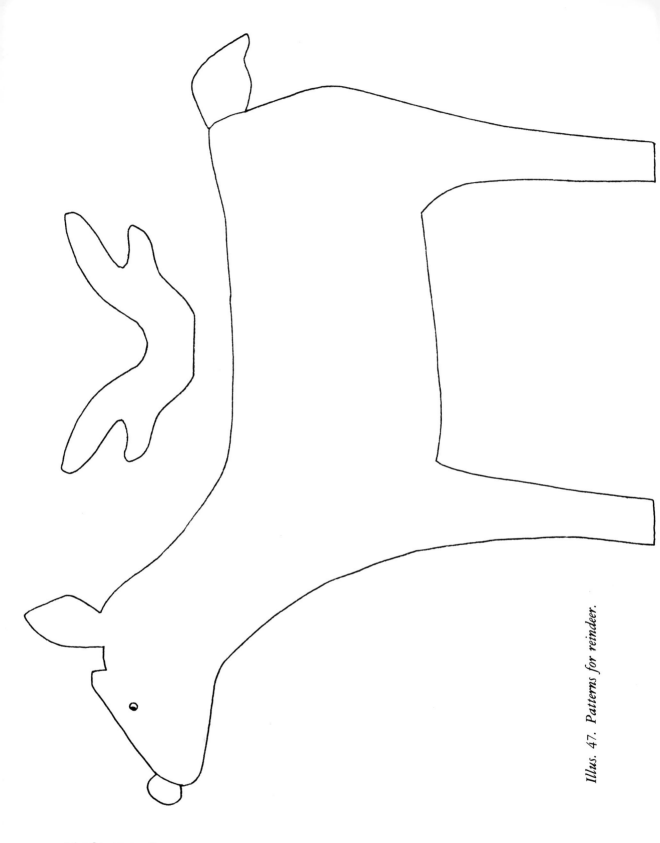

Illus. 47. Patterns for reindeer.

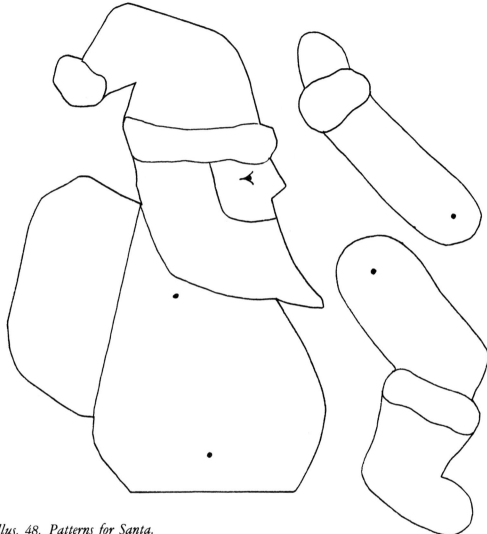

Illus. 48. Patterns for Santa.

patterns, and then trace reindeer and Santa body onto the ¾-in. wood. Trace arms and legs onto ⅜-in. wood, and antlers onto ¼-in. wood.

Cutting. Using a scroll saw or band saw, cut out all the above pieces, and then cut a 2 x 8½-in. base piece.

Drilling. Drill holes through Santa's body, arms, and legs using a ³⁄₃₂-in. bit (Illus. 49). See patterns for correct placement (Illus. 48).

Sanding. With either a stationary belt sander or a sanding wheel, sand edges of all pieces until a well-rounded look is achieved. Antlers, however, should be sanded by hand, and each piece should be

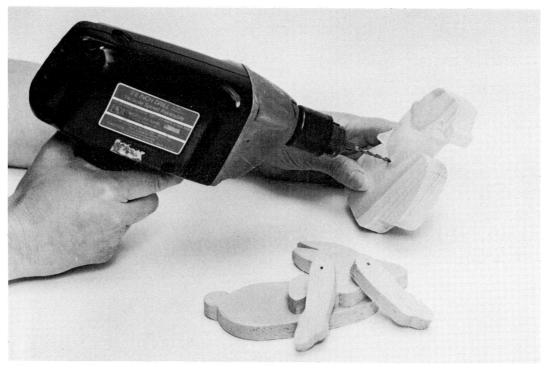

Illus. 49. Drilling holes in the body.

Illus. 50. Bending end of wire into a loop.

given a final hand-sanding with a fine-grade sandpaper.

Painting. Mix paints as listed below, keeping in mind that measurements are approximate.

Reindeer: 1 tsp. white / 1 tsp. burnt umber

Tail, beard, trim: 1 tsp. white / few drops burnt umber

Santa suit, nose: 1 tsp. red / few drops black

Antlers, bag: ½ tsp. raw umber

Boots: ¼ tsp. black

Base: 1 tsp. green / drop black

Reindeer eye: dot of white / dot of black

Assembling. Glue the reindeer to the base, and then glue the antlers in position.

Cut two 2¾-in. lengths of copper wire. With needle-nose pliers, bend one end of each wire into a small, closed loop. Attach arms and legs as shown in Illus. 46, and then bend the other end of each wire into a loop (Illus. 50). Tighten wires against the arms and legs to ensure good positioning.

Santa with Bag

Santa looks as though he's just getting ready to open his pack! This is a present-day interpretation of an American Santa. Use him with the sitting reindeer, along with some fresh greenery, for a nice grouping.

MATERIALS
Pine, ¾ in. thick: 6½ x 10 in.
Pine, ⅜ in. thick: 4 x 4 in.
Black felt: 4 x 10-in. piece
Copper wire, 14 gauge: 2¾-in. length
Acrylic paint: titanium white, mars black, naphthol red light, burnt umber
Wood glue
Sandpaper: medium and fine grades
Tracing paper
Poster board

TOOLS
Scroll saw or band saw
Stationary belt sander or sanding wheel
Drill with 3⁄32-in. bit
Needle-nose pliers

Illus. 51.

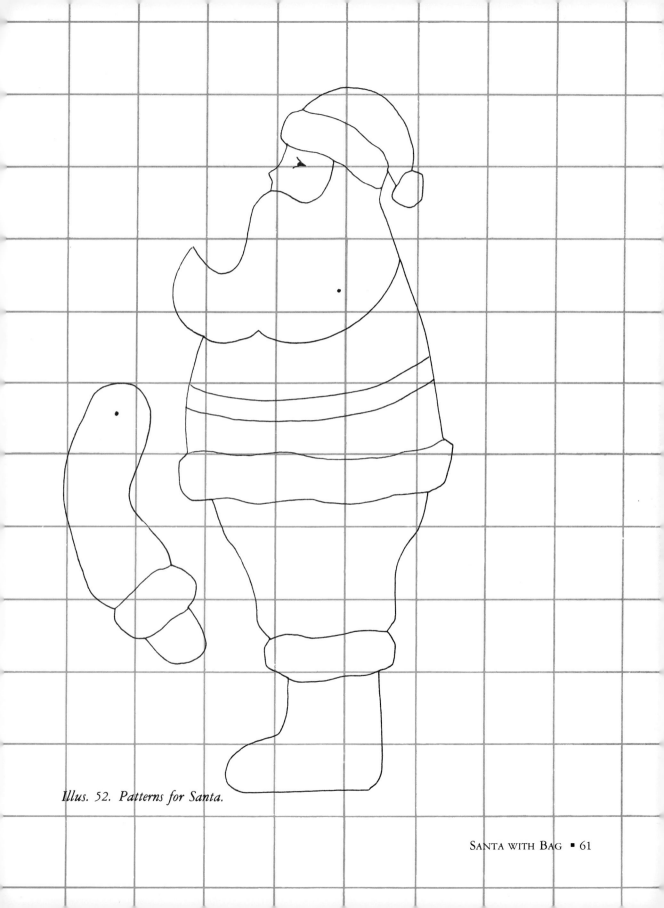

Illus. 52. Patterns for Santa.

Illus. 53. Cutting Santa's body with a scroll saw.

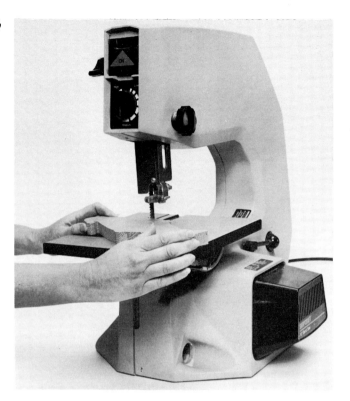

Illus. 54. Stitching lines for bag.

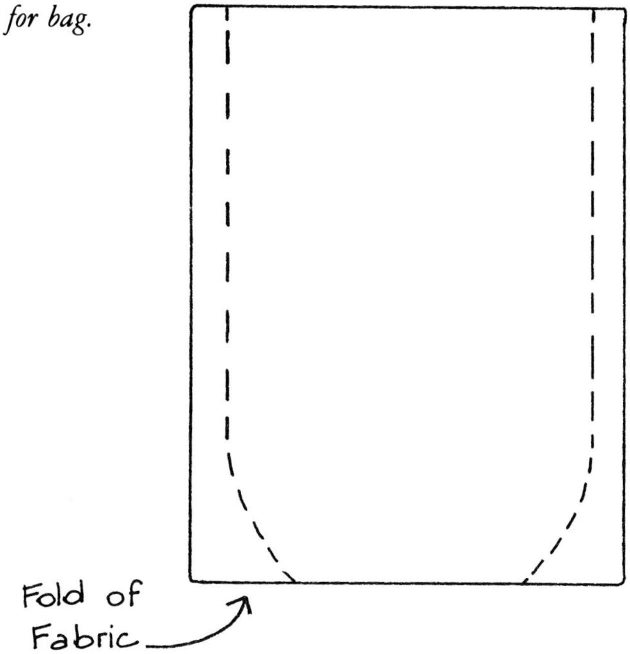

Fold of
Fabric

INSTRUCTIONS

Pattern. Trace pattern pieces and transfer onto poster board. Cut out poster-board patterns along outlines only; then trace Santa and draw a 3 x 3-in. base on ¾-in. wood. Trace arms onto ⅜-in. wood.

Cutting. With either a scroll saw or band saw, cut out all of the pieces for Santa. Use scissors to cut out the 4 x 10-in. piece of felt.

Drilling. Use a ³⁄₃₂-in. bit to drill a hole through the arms and body, as indicated on the patterns (Illus. 52).

Sanding. Sand and round all edges, using either a small stationary belt sander or sanding wheel. Give each piece a final sanding, by hand, with a fine-grade sandpaper.

Painting. Paint Santa with the following colors. Measurements are approximate.
Santa suit: 1 tsp. red / few drops black
Beard, trim: ¾ tsp. white / few drops burnt umber
Belt, boots, base: 1 tsp. black

Sewing. Fold the previously cut piece of black felt in half, lengthwise. By hand or machine, stitch the sides, using approximately ¼-in. seams. Taper the bottom (Illus. 54).

Turn felt right-side-out, and then take large stitches across the open top of the bag about one inch from the top (Illus. 55). Gather and knot.

Stitch a loop to hang the bag from Santa's hand.

Assembling. Cut a 2¾-in. piece of copper wire. Using needle-nose pliers, bend one end into a small, closed loop. Attach

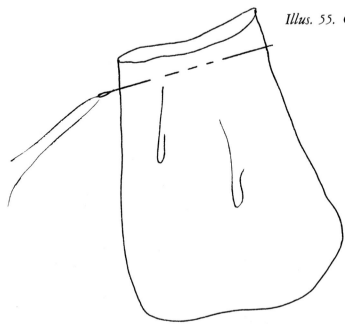

Illus. 55. Gathering stitches on bag.

the arms to the body, and then bend the other end into a small loop. Tighten the wires against the arms to ensure good positioning.

Glue Santa to the center of the base and, when dry, hang the bag on one of his hands.

Sitting reindeer with Christmas tree, floppy dog, and lamb with watermelon.

Floppy cats—perfect for Halloween!

Uncle Sam.

American Indian.

Jester and monkey acrobats.

Bride & groom.

B

Gnome with cart and smaller gnome.

"Sky-high" animals.

Rabbit with cart filled with Easter eggs.

C

Santa, sleigh, and reindeer.

Nativity scene.

D

Santa & Sleigh

Use Santa and his sleigh as a unique centerpiece with greenery and miniature presents (wrap small blocks of wood), or use Santa and his sleigh with a team of reindeer to ride across the fireplace mantel.

MATERIALS

Pine, ¾ in. thick: 3½ x 5½ in.
Pine, ⅜ in. thick: 8 x 18 in.
Birch plywood, ¼ in. thick: 5 x 6 in.
Copper wire, 14 gauge: 2¾ in.
Wood glue
Acrylic paint: titanium white, naphthol red light, permanent green deep, mars black, burnt umber
Stain: medium color
Sandpaper: medium and fine grades
Tracing paper
Poster board

TOOLS

Scroll saw or band saw
Stationary belt sander or sanding wheel
Drill with ³⁄₃₂-in. bit (optional, ¼-in. bit)
Needle-nose pliers

INSTRUCTIONS

Pattern. Trace pattern pieces and transfer onto poster board. Cut out poster-board patterns, and then trace Santa body onto ¾-in. wood. Trace the tree and sleigh bottom onto ¼-in. wood. Remaining patterns should be traced onto ⅜-in. wood. Treat reindeer patterns as you treated reindeer patterns for Santa on Reindeer.

Cutting. All pieces may be cut with either a scroll saw or band saw. The sleigh and runners can be cut as one piece if you have access to a scroll saw. To do this, drill a ¼-in. hole into the inside runner area, which will be discarded, in order to insert the blade. Otherwise, cut out the sleigh along the dotted line to free the

Illus. 56. Reindeer. See pages 55–59 for instructions on making the reindeer.

Illus. 57. Santa and sleigh.

65

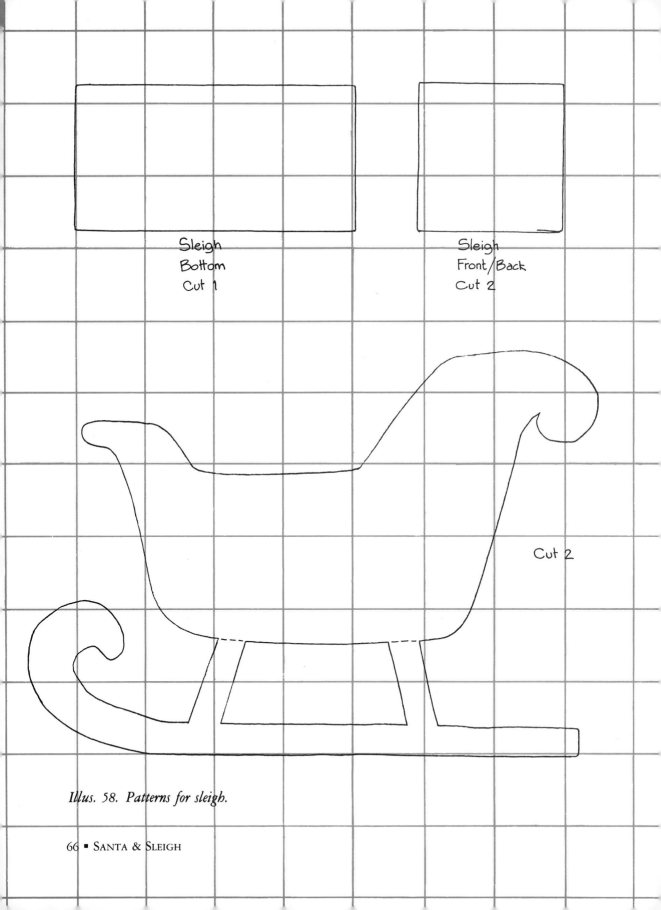

Sleigh
Bottom
Cut 1

Sleigh
Front/Back
Cut 2

Cut 2

Illus. 58. Patterns for sleigh.

Cut 2

Illus. 59. Patterns for Santa and Christmas tree.

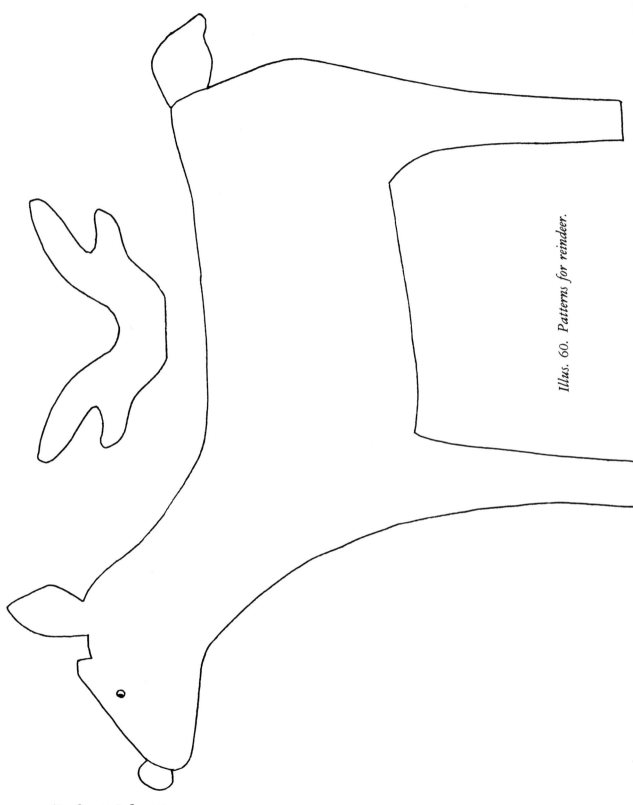

Illus. 60. Patterns for reindeer.

runner piece. The runner piece can be glued in place later.

Drilling. Using a ³⁄₃₂-in. bit, drill through the body and arms of Santa, as indicated on the pattern (Illus. 59).

Sanding. Except for the front and back pieces of the sleigh, round all edges using either a stationary belt sander or sanding wheel. Sand areas that are hard to reach by hand.

Round only the top edges of the front and back sleigh pieces (Illus. 61). The remaining edges have to be straight in order to have a good gluing surface.

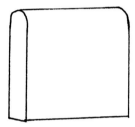

Illus. 61. Detail of front and back sleigh pieces.

Give all pieces a final sanding, by hand, with a fine-grade sandpaper.

Gluing. Glue the sides of the sleigh to the front and back pieces. See Illus. 62 for the proper gluing position. When dry, glue the bottom in place.

If the runners have to be glued, do so at this time, making sure they are lined up evenly.

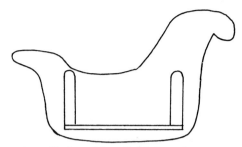

Illus. 62. Gluing sides of sleigh to front and back pieces of sleigh.

Painting. Paint Santa and his sleigh with the following mixtures of paint. Remember that measurements are approximate.
Tree: ½ tsp. green / drop of black
Beard, trim: ½ tsp. white / drop of burnt umber
Santa suit: ½ tsp. red / drop of black
Sleigh: ½ tsp. red / drop of black (watered down)
Runners: medium-color stain, applied with a small brush

Assembling. Cut a 2¾-in. length of copper wire. Using needle-nose pliers, bend one end into a small, closed loop. Attach the arms, and then bend the other end of the wire into a closed loop. Tighten the loops against the arms to ensure good positioning.

Set Santa in the sleigh along with the tree.

Religious
Folk Figures

Jesus, Mary & Joseph

These folk art figures depict the traditional biblical scene of Mary and Joseph fleeing with the baby Jesus.

MATERIALS
Pine, ¾ in. thick: 10 x 14 in.
Pine, ⅜ in. thick: 4 x 4 in.
Wooden dowel, ³⁄₁₆-in. diameter: 7 in.
Copper wire, 14 gauge: 3 in.
Jute twine: 3 ft.
Acrylic paint: titanium white, cerulean blue hue, burnt umber, naphthol red light, mars black
Sandpaper: medium and fine grades
Tracing paper
Poster board

TOOLS
Scroll saw or band saw
Drill with ³⁄₃₂-, ³⁄₁₆-, ⅛-in. bits
Stationary belt sander or sanding wheel
Needle-nose pliers

INSTRUCTIONS

Pattern. Trace pattern and transfer onto poster board. Cut out along outlines, and then trace both large patterns onto ¾-in. wood. Trace pattern for arms onto ⅜-in. wood. Lightly pencil in detail lines.

Cutting. With either a scroll saw or band saw, cut out the above pieces along the outlines. Cut a 7-in.-long, ³⁄₁₆-in.-diameter, wooden dowel.

Drilling. Drill a hole through the torso and shoulders of arm pieces with the ³⁄₃₂-

Illus. 63.

Illus. 64. Pattern for baby Jesus, Mary, and donkey.

Illus. 65. Patterns for Joseph.

in. bit, as indicated on the patterns (Illus. 65). Use the ⅛-in. bit to drill a hole through the front of one of the hands. Finally, drill a hole through the front of the other hand using the 3⁄16-in. bit.

Sanding. Sand all pieces with either a small stationary belt sander or the sanding wheel. Sand the staff (wooden dowel) so that it has gouges in it to make it look like a worn stick.

Give all pieces a final sanding, by hand, with a fine-grade sandpaper.

Painting. Paint the figures with the following paints. Remember that the measurements given are approximate.
Joseph's robe, blanket, Mary's shoes: ½ tsp. red / ¾ tsp. burnt umber
Mary's robe, trim, Joseph's robe: ½ tsp. blue / ¼ tsp. black / ¼ tsp. white

Mary's head covering: ⅛ tsp. blue / ⅛ tsp. white / few drops black
Baby Jesus, donkey's tail: ½ tsp. white / few drops burnt umber
Donkey: ½ tsp. burnt umber / ½ tsp. white
Beard, Joseph's shoe: slightly watered-down burnt umber
Faces, hands: very watered-down burnt umber
Donkey's eye: dot of white / dot of black
Paint or draw eyes for Jesus, Mary, and Joseph.

Assembling. Cut a 3-in. piece of copper wire. Using needle-nose pliers, bend one end into a small, closed loop. Slide the straight end into Joseph's arm, body, and then the other arm. Bend the remaining end of wire into another closed loop.

Illus. 66. Back view of paint lines.

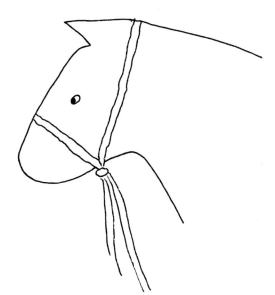

Illus. 67. Tying jute to donkey.

Tighten against the body for good positioning of the arms.

Next, cut a 3-ft. piece of jute. Place the center of the jute at a point just behind the donkey's ears. Wrap this around the neck, cross the strings, and wrap around the nose. Knot the jute under the neck to hold securely (Illus. 67). Approximately 5 in. from the knot, make a second knot to tie the strings together. Cut one of the strings at the knot. Slip the jute into the hand of Joseph and knot it on the other side. Cut off excess.

Slide the staff into Joseph's other hand and they're ready for their journey.

Nativity

Since wooden Nativity sets are extremely hard to acquire, this folk art interpretation should be very collectible, and will be much appreciated by any fortunate recipient of your handiwork.

For convenience, instructions are given for 3 different groupings: three-piece Nativity, three Wise Men, and camels.

Three-Piece Nativity

MATERIALS
Pine, ¾ in. thick: 8 x 8 in.
Pine, ⅜ in. thick: 4 x 5 in.
Birch plywood, ¼ in. thick: 4 x 10 in.
Copper wire, 14 gauge: 6 in.
Acrylic paint: titanium white, burnt umber, red oxide, cerulean blue hue, mars black, raw umber
Stain: light color
Wood glue
Sandpaper: medium and fine grades
Tracing paper
Poster board

TOOLS
Scroll saw or band saw
Stationary belt sander or sanding wheel
Drill with ³⁄₃₂-in. bit
Needle-nose pliers

INSTRUCTIONS
Pattern. Trace pattern pieces and transfer onto poster board. Cut out poster-board patterns, and then trace crib pieces onto

Illus. 68.

Illus. 69. Body patterns for Joseph and Mary.

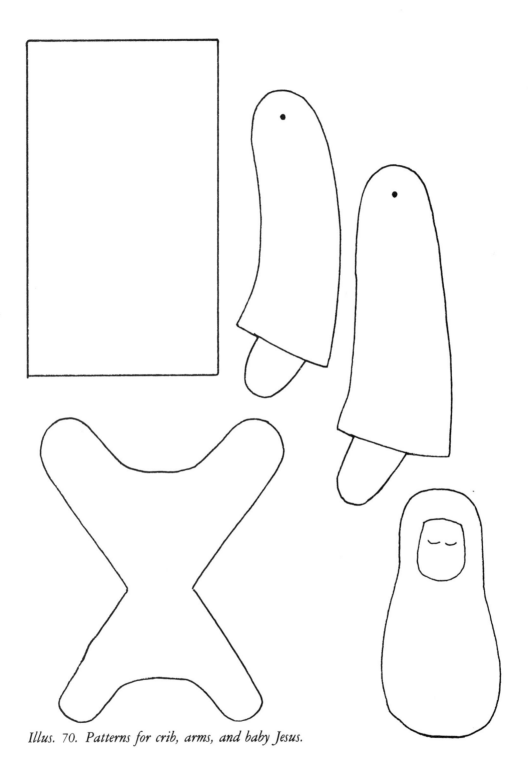

Illus. 70. Patterns for crib, arms, and baby Jesus.

¼-in. wood. Trace arms onto ⅜-in. wood and all remaining pieces onto ¾-in. wood.

Cutting. With either a band saw or scroll saw, cut out all the pieces for the Nativity.

Drilling. Use a 3/32-in. bit to drill holes into the arms of Mary and Joseph. Also drill through the shoulder area of the bodies, as indicated on the patterns (Illus. 69).

Sanding. Using either a stationary belt sander or sanding wheel, sand the edges of all pieces until well rounded. Then give each piece a final sanding, by hand, with a fine-grade sandpaper.

Gluing. Set one end piece of the crib on a flat surface. Spread a thin layer of glue on one end of each side section and glue to the crib end (Illus. 71). Do not use

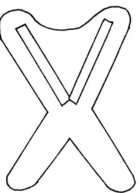

Illus. 71. Gluing positions of side sections.

too much glue or it will ooze out and the area will not stain properly. If this does occur, wipe area immediately with a damp

cloth and, when dry, sand to remove as much glue as possible.

When glue has dried, glue the opposite end in place, following the same procedures.

Painting. Paint the figures with the following mixtures. Measurements are approximate.
Baby Jesus, Joseph's head covering: 1 tsp. white / few drops burnt umber
Joseph's robe: 1 tsp. red oxide
Mary's head covering: ¼ tsp. blue / ⅛ tsp. white / few drops black
Mary's robe: ½ tsp. blue / ¼ tsp. white / ⅛ tsp. black

Staining. Apply a medium-color stain to the crib with either a brush or a small rag. Remove any excess stain with a cloth to avoid streaking. Set the crib aside to dry.

Assembling. Cut two 2¾-in. lengths of copper wire. Using needle-nose pliers, bend one end of each wire into a small, closed loop. Attach the arms for each figure, and then bend the other end of the wires into a small loop. Tighten the loops against the arms to ensure good positioning.

Three Wise Men

MATERIALS
Pine, ¾ in. thick: 8 x 18 in.
Pine, ⅜ in. thick: 6½ x 9 in.
Copper wire, 14 gauge: 9-in. length

Acrylic paint: titanium white, burnt umber, permanent green deep, naphthol red light, cerulean blue hue, raw umber, thalo bronze
Sandpaper: medium and fine grades
Tracing paper
Poster board

TOOLS

Scroll saw or band saw
Stationary belt sander or sanding wheel
Drill with ³⁄₃₂-in. bit
Needle-nose pliers

INSTRUCTIONS

Pattern. Trace pattern pieces and transfer to poster board. Cut poster-board patterns, and then trace bodies of the Wise Men onto ¾-in. wood. Trace the arms onto ⅜-in. wood.

Cutting. Use either a scroll saw or band saw to cut out all the above pieces.

Drilling. With the ³⁄₃₂-in. bit, drill a hole through each Wise Man and his arms. Location for drilling is designated on each pattern piece (Illus. 73 and 74). Also drill a hole into one hand of Wise Man 1 (purple robe) and Wise Man 2 (green robe).

Sanding. Sand each piece until edges are rounded. Use a stationary belt sander or sanding wheel.

Give each piece a final sanding, by hand, with a fine-grade paper.

Painting. Paint the Wise Men as shown on page D of the color section. Approximate proportions for paint mixtures are listed below.
Trim: 1 tsp. white / few drops burnt umber
Robe, Wise Man 1 (kneeling): ½ tsp. red / ½ tsp. blue

Illus. 72. Three Wise Men. See pages 84–88 for instructions on making the camels.

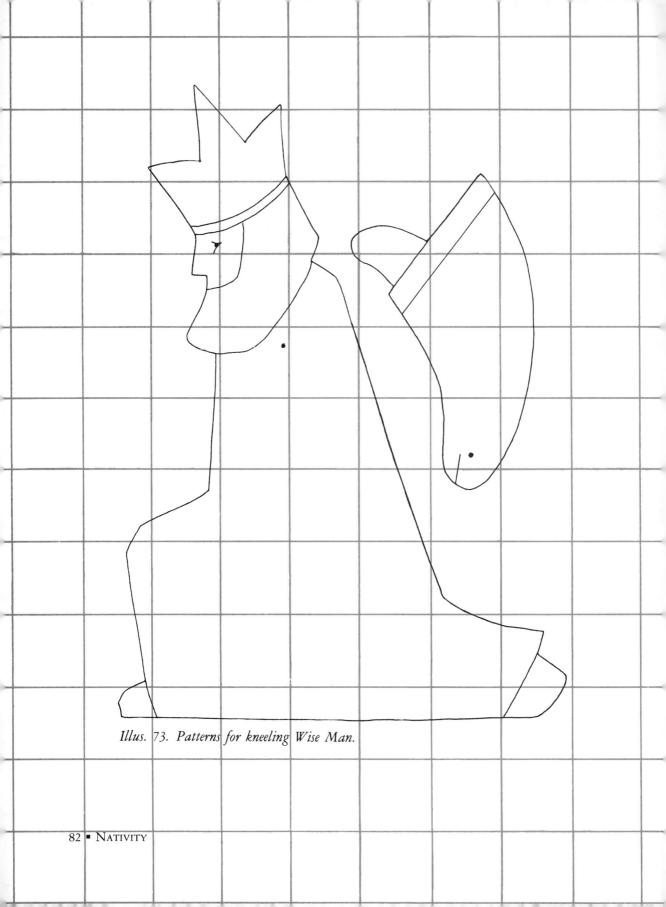

Illus. 73. Patterns for kneeling Wise Man.

Illus. 74. Patterns for Wise Men.

Robe, Wise Man 2: 1 tsp. green / few
drops black
Robe, Wise Man 3: 1 tsp. red / few drops
black
Beard, Wise Man 3: ¼ tsp. black
Beard, Wise Men, 1, 2: watered-down
burnt umber
Crowns: 1 tsp. bronze

Assembling. Cut three 2¾-in. lengths of
copper wire. Using needle-nose pliers,
bend one end of each wire into a small,
closed loop. Attach the arms for each
Wise Man, and then bend the other end
of each wire into a small loop. Tighten
the loops against the arms to ensure good
positioning.

Thread jute ropes from the camels
through the hands of Wise Men 1 and 2,
and then knot them.

Camels

MATERIALS

Pine, ¾ in. thick: 12 x 24 in.
Birch plywood, ¼ in. thick: 3 x 3 in.
Copper wire, 14 gauge: 10 in.
Black steel wire, 16 gauge: 8 in.
Brass bells, ⅜-in. diameter: 16
Acrylic paint: naphthol red light, perma-
nent green deep, cerulean blue hue, mars
black, titanium white
Stain: light color
Jute twine: 24 in.
Sandpaper: medium and fine grades
Tracing paper
Poster board

TOOLS

Scroll saw or band saw
Stationary belt sander or sanding wheel
Drill with 1/16-in. bit
Needle-nose pliers

INSTRUCTIONS

Pattern. Trace both pattern pieces and
transfer onto poster board. Cut out poster-
board patterns, and then trace both
camels onto the ¾-in. wood. Make sure
the standing camel is traced onto the
wood with the legs following the grain of
the wood. This will reduce possible break-
age.

Trace the ears onto the ¼-in. wood.

Cutting. Cut all pieces out with either a
scroll saw or band saw. Be extremely careful while cutting out the ears. If possible,
these should be cut with a tabletop scroll
saw.

Drilling. Using the 1/16-in. bit, drill 4
holes through the side of each camel.
These are for the wires that hold the
bells.

Sanding. Sand all edges until well
rounded, using either a small, stationary
belt sander or a sanding wheel. Use extreme care while sanding the legs of the
standing camel, since they are rather thin.

Painting/Staining. Paint the blankets of
the camels as follows. Remember that
measurements are approximate.
Blanket, standing camel: ½ tsp.
red / drop of black

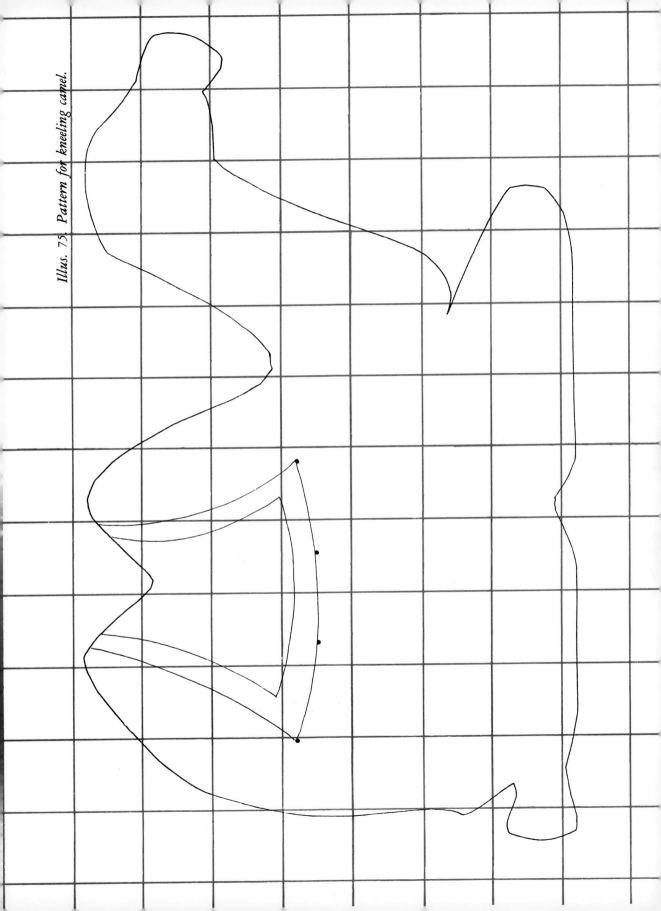

Illus. 75. Pattern for kneeling camel.

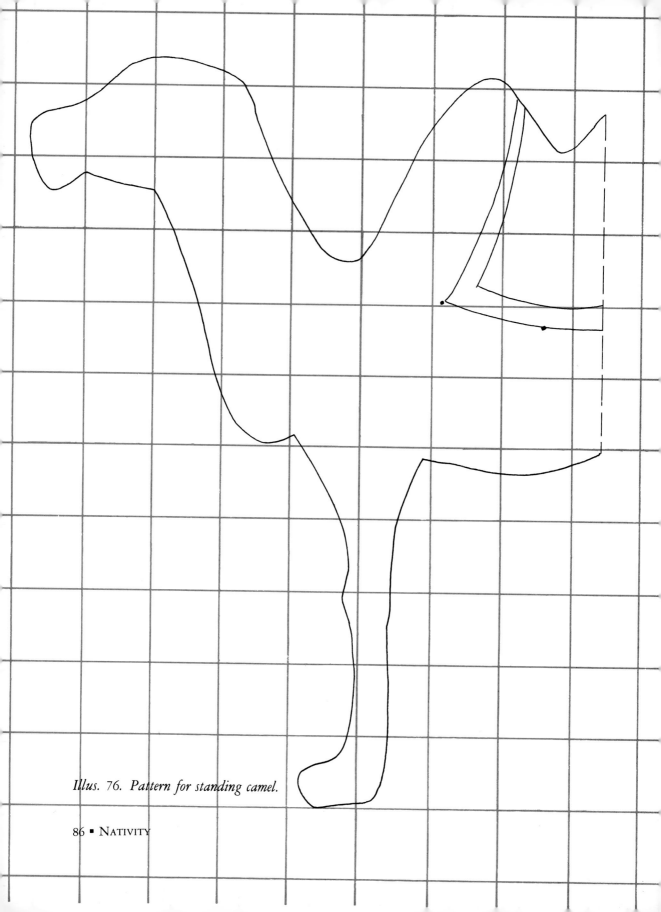

Illus. 76. Pattern for standing camel.

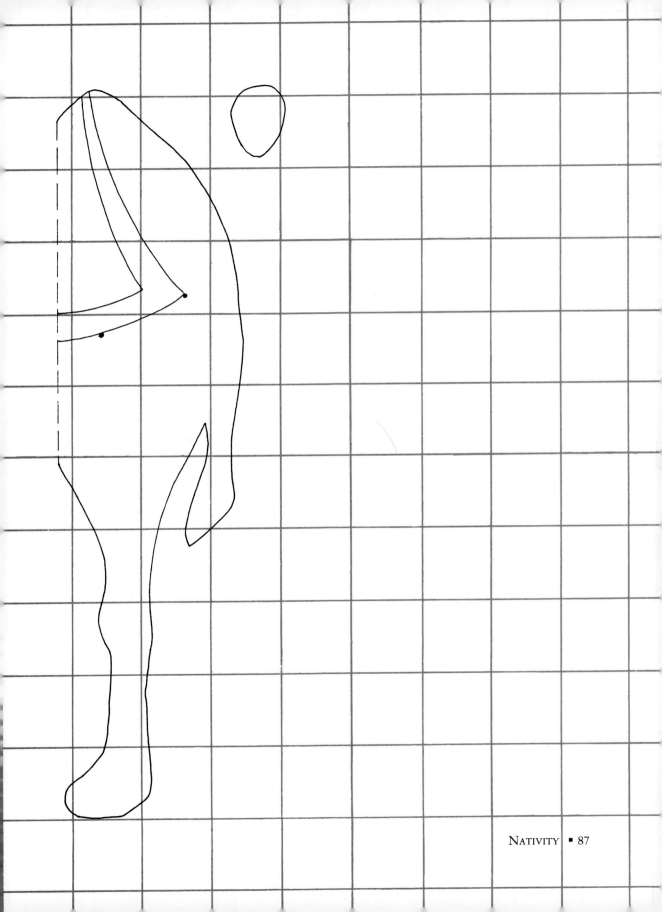

Trim, standing camel: ¼ tsp. green / drop of black
Blanket, resting camel: ¼ tsp. red / ¼ tsp. blue
Trim, resting camel: ¼ tsp. red / drop of black
Eyes: dot of white / dot of black

When paint has completely dried, stain the camels with a light-color stain. Apply with a cloth and immediately wipe off any excess. Stain may be applied over top of the paint.

Assembling. Cut eight 2-in. lengths of steel wire and two 4-in. lengths of copper wire. Using needle-nose pliers, bend one end of each piece of steel wire, enclosing a bell (Illus. 77), into a small, closed loop. Slide the wires through the holes in the camels, and then attach another bell on the other side, while bending the end into a loop.

Illus. 77.

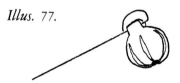

Illus. 78.

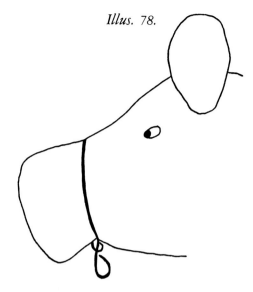

After all bells have been attached, bend a 4-in. length of copper wire around the muzzle of each camel. Twist ends of copper wire to form a loop for the jute leash (Illus. 78).

Glue the ears in place, and the camels are finished. Attach a 12-in. piece of jute to each camel.

Sill Sitters

Angel Sill-Sitter

Make this folk art angel to watch over any room. Place her on the mantel, a window sill, or on a shelf.

MATERIALS
Pine, ¾ in. thick: 8 x 10 in.
Stain: light color
Acrylic paint: titanium white, burnt umber, naphthol red light, turner's yellow, mars black
Wood glue
Sandpaper: medium and fine grades
Tracing paper
Poster board

TOOLS
Scroll saw or band saw
Stationary belt sander or sanding wheel
Woodcarving tool: ¼-in. flat chisel (optional)
Small C-clamp (G-cramp), if carving detail

INSTRUCTIONS

Pattern. Trace each pattern piece, and then transfer onto poster board. Cut out patterns along the outlines and trace onto the wood. Lightly sketch details with a pencil.

Cutting. Using a scroll saw or band saw, cut out the 3 angel pieces. Only cut along the outlines.

Carving. (Optional) If you wish to have a more dimensional look, use a small carving chisel. Practise on scrap wood if you

Illus. 79.

have never done any carving. Always clamp your workpiece down and keep your hands behind the blade at all times.

Define entire detail by pressing the chisel straight into the wood about ⅛ in. deep (Illus. 82). Do this in a continuous line; then go over all details again by placing the chisel 1/16 in. from the incised line (chisel should be held at a 45° angle, as shown in Illus. 83), and then pressing into the wood to meet the first cut. Continue around the design.

Sanding. Use the belt sander or sanding wheel to round all outside edges of each piece. Give a final sanding, by hand, with a fine-grade sandpaper. Carefully sand carved details.

Gluing. Attach the body pieces with glue, as indicated in Illus. 84. Let the assembly dry thoroughly before handling.

Painting. Paint the angel with the following paints. Measurements are approximate.
Dress: 1 tsp. white / drop of black
Duck body: ¼ tsp. white
Hair: ¼ tsp. yellow / drop of burnt umber

Ribbon: ⅛ tsp. red / drop of black
Duck beak, legs: ⅛ tsp. yellow / drop of red / drop of burnt umber

Staining. Apply a light-color stain over the entire angel. Wipe off any excess and set aside to dry.

Illus. 80. Top body pattern for angel.

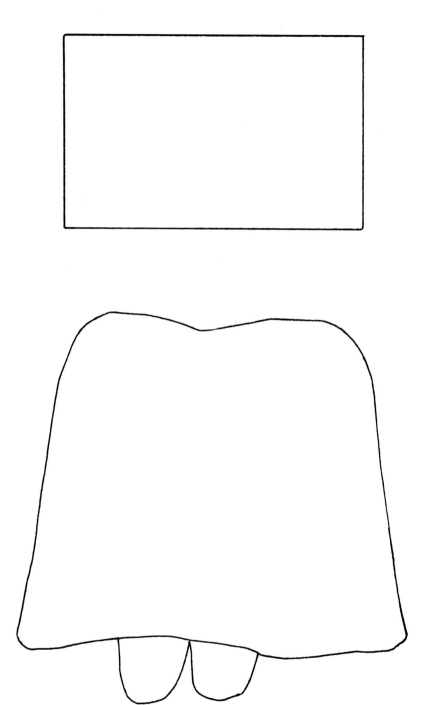

Illus. 81. Lower body pattern for angel and pattern for midsection.

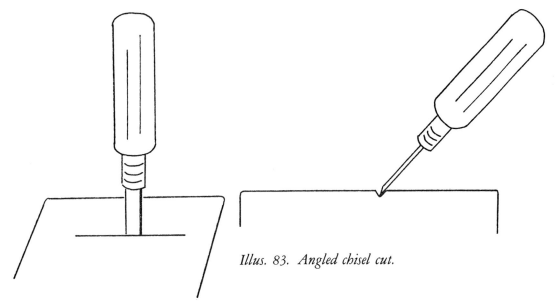

Illus. 82. Straight chisel cut.

Illus. 83. Angled chisel cut.

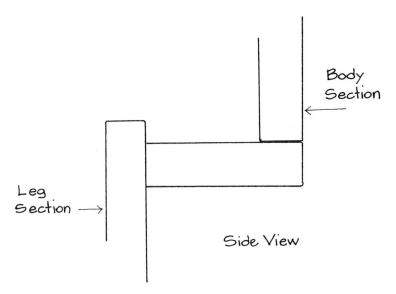

Body
Section

Leg
Section →

Side View

Illus. 84. Gluing positions of body pieces.

Santa Sill-Sitter

This easy-to-make Santa will "sit" on the mantel to guard all the Christmas stockings.

MATERIALS

Pine, ¾ in. thick: 8 x 14 in.
Acrylic paint: mars black, naphthol red light, permanent green deep, titanium white
Wood glue
Sandpaper: medium and fine grades
Tracing paper
Poster board

Illus. 85.

TOOLS

Scroll saw or band saw
Stationary belt sander or sanding wheel
Wood-carving tool: ¼-in. flat chisel (optional)
Small C-clamp (G-cramp), if carving details

INSTRUCTIONS

Pattern. Trace each pattern piece, and then transfer onto poster board. Cut out patterns, along outlines, and trace them onto the ¾-in. wood. Lightly draw the details, such as the beard and bag, onto the wood in pencil.

Cutting. Use a scroll saw or band saw to

Illus. 86. Top body pattern for Santa.

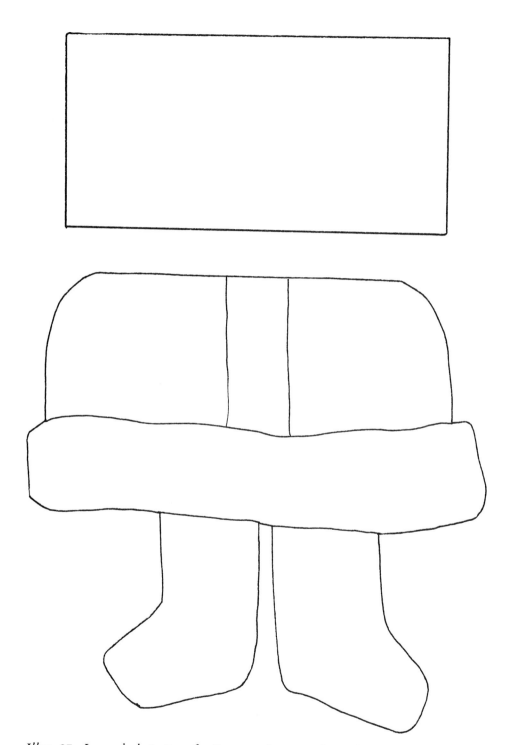

Illus. 87. Lower body pattern for Santa and pattern for midsection.

cut the pieces for Santa. Only cut along the outlines.

Carving. (Optional) For a more dimensional look, carve details with a small carving chisel.

If you have never done any carving previously, practise on some scrap wood. Always clamp your workpiece down and keep your hands behind the blade at all times.

Carve detail by first pressing the chisel straight into the wood about ⅛ in. deep (Illus. 82, on page 93). Do this in a continuous line. Go over all details again by placing the chisel ¹⁄₁₆ in. from the incised line (chisel should be held at a 45° angle, as shown in Illus. 83, on page 93), and then pressing into the wood to meet the first cut. Continue around the design.

Sanding. Using the belt sander or sanding wheel, sand all edges until rounded. Give each piece a final sanding, by hand, with a fine-grade sandpaper. Carefully hand-sand carved details.

Gluing. Attach the body pieces with glue as indicated in Illus. 84 on page 93. Let them dry thoroughly before handling.

Painting. Paint the Santa with the following paints. Remember that measurements are approximate. Adjust as desired.
Santa's coat: 2 tsp. red / few drops black
Beard, fur trim, eyebrows: 1½ tsp. white
Bag: ½ tsp. green / drop black
Boots: ½ tsp. black
Paint eyes with black, and color cheeks with very watered-down red.

Folk Toys

Floppy Rabbit

This little, jointed rabbit will delight any age group, and he's just the right size for an Easter basket!

MATERIALS
Pine, ⅜ in. thick: 6 x 12 in.
Copper wire, 14 gauge: 6 in.
Acrylic paint: titanium white, burnt umber, mars black
Sandpaper: medium and fine grades
Tracing paper
Poster board

TOOLS
Scroll saw or band saw
Stationary belt sander or sanding wheel
Drill with ³⁄₃₂-in. bit
Needle-nose pliers

INSTRUCTIONS

Pattern. Trace pattern pieces and transfer onto poster board. Cut out patterns, and then trace each piece onto ⅜-in. wood.

Cutting. Use a band saw or scroll saw to cut out all the rabbit pieces.

Drilling. With the ³⁄₃₂-in. bit, drill holes in the legs and body as indicated on the patterns (Illus. 89). Drill holes as straight as possible to ensure good movement.

Sanding. Using a small stationary belt sander or sanding wheel, sand all edges, rounding smoothly. Give each piece a final sanding, by hand, with a fine-grade sandpaper.

Illus. 88.

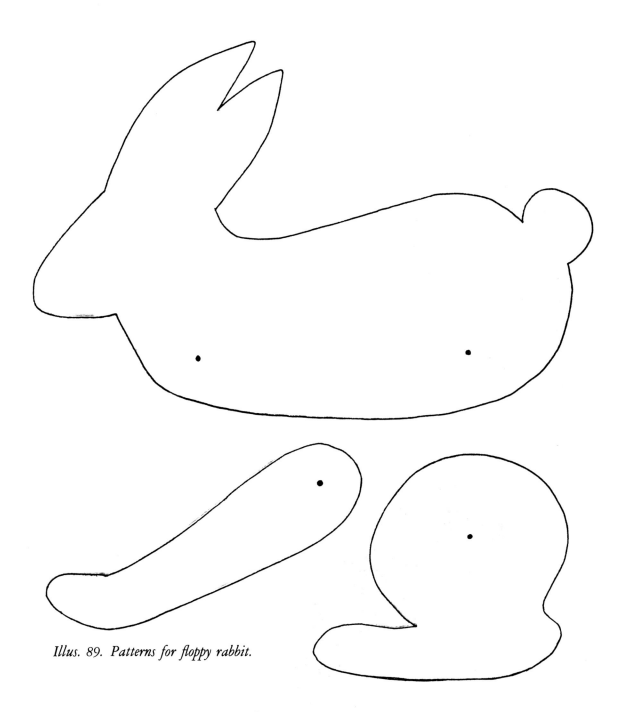

Illus. 89. Patterns for floppy rabbit.

Illus. 90. Sanding rabbit piece.

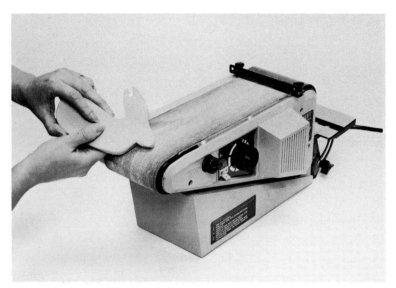

Painting. To paint the rabbit, mix approximately one tsp. white with a few drops of burnt umber. This will produce an off-white color. Paint all pieces and set them aside to dry before attempting to assemble.

Assembling. Cut 2 pieces of copper wire, each 2¾ in. long. Using needle-nose pliers, bend one end of each wire into a small, closed loop. Slide the straight ends through the legs and body, as shown in Illus. 91, and then bend the remaining

Illus. 91. Inserting wire through legs and body.

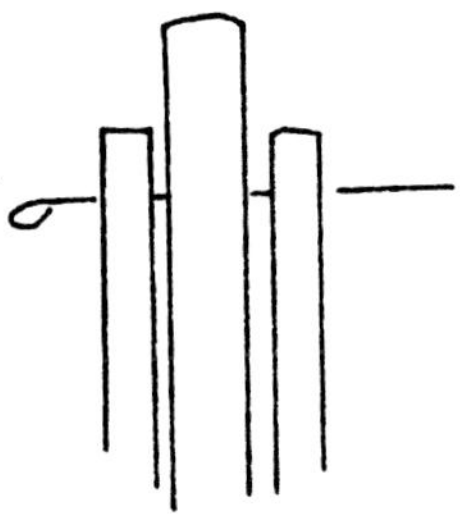

straight ends into closed loops also. Do not tighten wires too much, as the rabbit should be able to "flop" around!

Floppy Cat

This is the perfect gift for your favorite cat lover—a cat that stretches his hind legs, his front legs, or just stretches out! For fun, make a trio of different-colored cats.

MATERIALS

Pine, ⅜ in. thick: 6 x 8 in.
Copper wire, 14 gauge: 6 in.
Acrylic paint: mars black, titanium white
Sandpaper: medium and fine grades
Tracing paper
Poster board

TOOLS

Scroll saw or band saw
Stationary belt sander or sanding wheel
Drill with ³⁄₃₂-in. bit
Needle-nose pliers

INSTRUCTIONS

Pattern. Trace pattern pieces and transfer onto poster board. Cut out poster-board patterns, and then trace onto the ⅜-in. wood.

Cutting. With either a scroll saw or band saw, cut out all pieces for the cat.

Drilling. Drill holes into each piece using a ³⁄₃₂-in. bit. See pattern (Illus. 93) for drilling guide.

Sanding. Use a stationary belt sander or a sanding wheel to round all of the edges. Carefully sand around the tail; then give each piece a final sanding, by hand, using a fine-grade paper.

Painting. Paint the entire cat black (approximately ¾ tsp. paint) or any other desired color. When dry, paint a dot of white for the eye, and then paint a

Illus. 92.

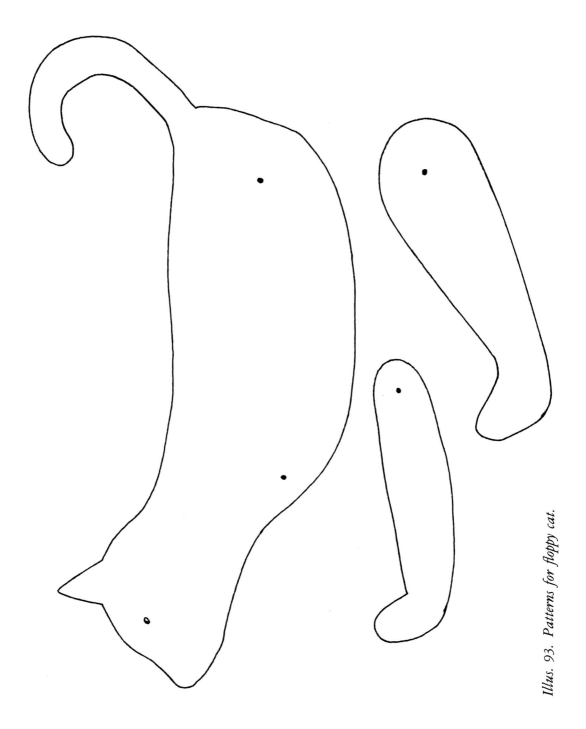

smaller dot of black on top of the white one.

Assembling. Cut two 2¾-in. pieces of copper wire. Using needle-nose pliers, bend one end of each wire into a small, closed loop. Attach the legs as shown in Illus. 94; then bend the other ends of the wires into small, closed loops. Do not tighten the wires, as the cat should be free to move.

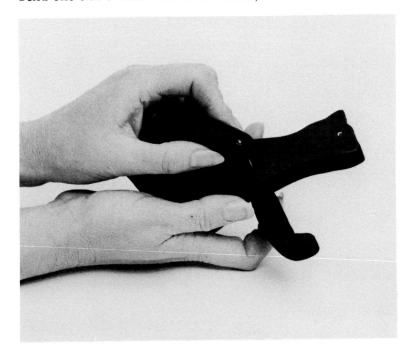

Illus. 94. Attaching cat's legs.

Floppy Dog

This floppy little dog can be posed in many different positions.

MATERIALS
Pine, ⅜ in. thick: 5 x 7 in.
Copper wire, 14 gauge: 6 in.
Acrylic paint: titanium white, burnt umber, mars black
Sandpaper: medium and fine grades
Tracing paper
Poster board

TOOLS
Scroll saw or band saw
Drill with ³⁄₃₂-in. bit
Stationary belt sander or sanding wheel
Needle-nose pliers

INSTRUCTIONS

Pattern. Trace pattern pieces and transfer onto poster board. Cut out poster-board patterns, and then trace onto the ⅜-in. wood. Be sure to trace 2 of each leg.

Cutting. Using a scroll saw or band saw, cut out the above pieces.

Drilling. With the ³⁄₃₂-in. bit, drill holes into the body and legs, as indicated on the patterns (Illus. 96).

Sanding. Sand the edges of all pieces

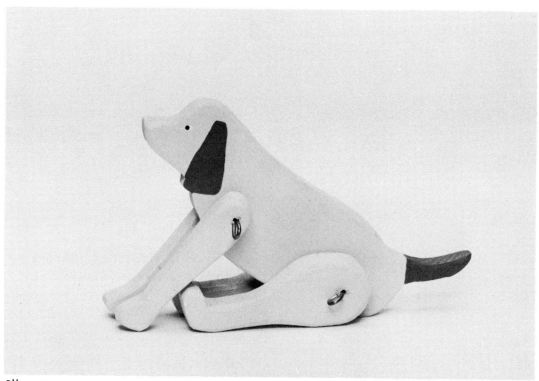

Illus. 95.

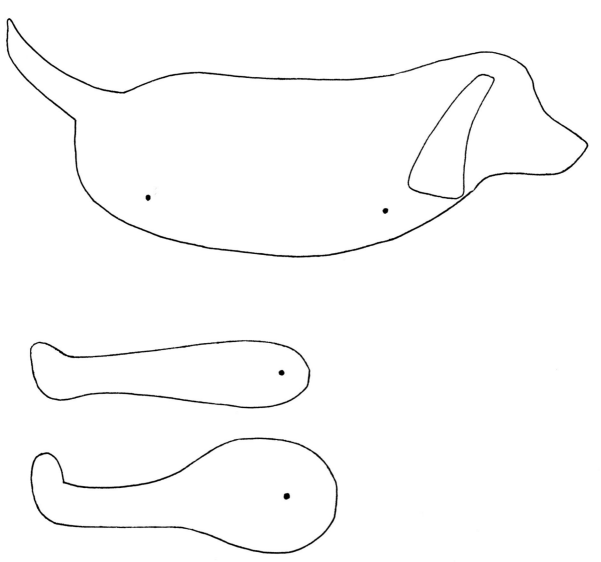

Illus. 96. Patterns for floppy dog.

until rounded. This will give the dog a carved appearance. Give each piece a final sanding, by hand, with a fine-grade paper.

Painting. Mix a few drops of burnt umber with approximately ½ tsp. of white. Paint the legs and body of the dog this color.

Mix a few more drops of burnt umber with the remaining paint already mixed. This should make a medium-brown color. Paint the ears and tail with this mixture.

Paint a dot of white for the eye. When dry, paint a smaller dot of black inside the white dot.

Assembling. Cut 2 pieces of copper wire approximately 2¾ in. long. Using needle-nose pliers, bend one end of each wire into a closed loop. Slide the straight end of the wire through the legs and body, and then use the pliers to bend the other end into a loop. Joints should be loose to enable free movement of legs.

Rabbit with Cart

Rabbits are traditionally identified with Easter, but this one can be used year-round. Fill his cart with jelly beans for Easter, hearts for Valentine's Day, and miniature presents for Christmas.

MATERIALS
Pine, ¾ in. thick: 3 x 7 in.
Pine, ⅜ in. thick: 4 x 10 in.
Birch plywood, ¼ in. thick: 8 x 12 in.
Wooden dowel, ⅛-in. diameter: 6 in.
Copper wire, 14 gauge: 6 in.
Acrylic paint: titanium white, burnt umber, naphthol red light, mars black, permanent green deep
Wood glue
Sandpaper: medium and fine grades
Tracing paper
Poster board

TOOLS
Scroll saw or band saw
Stationary belt sander or sanding wheel
Drill with ³⁄₃₂-, ⅛-, ⁵⁄₃₂-in. bits
Needle-nose pliers

INSTRUCTIONS

Pattern. Trace all pattern pieces and transfer onto poster board. Cut out poster-board patterns, and then trace the body of

Illus. 97.

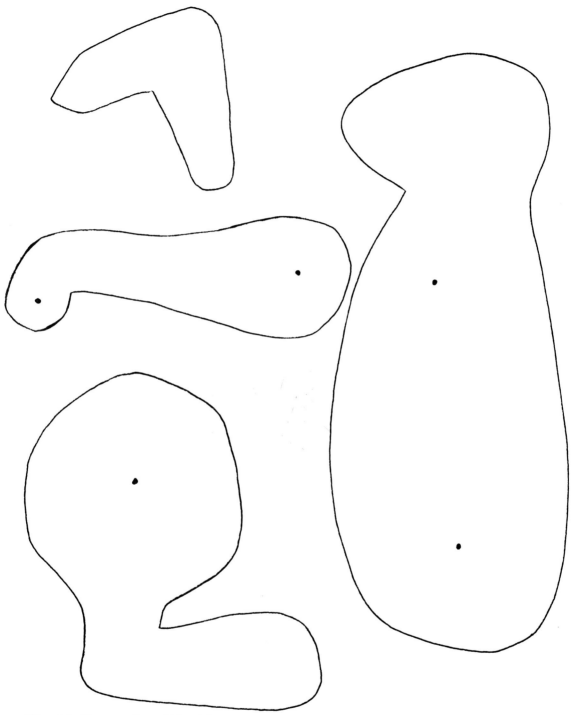

Illus. 98. Patterns for rabbit with cart.

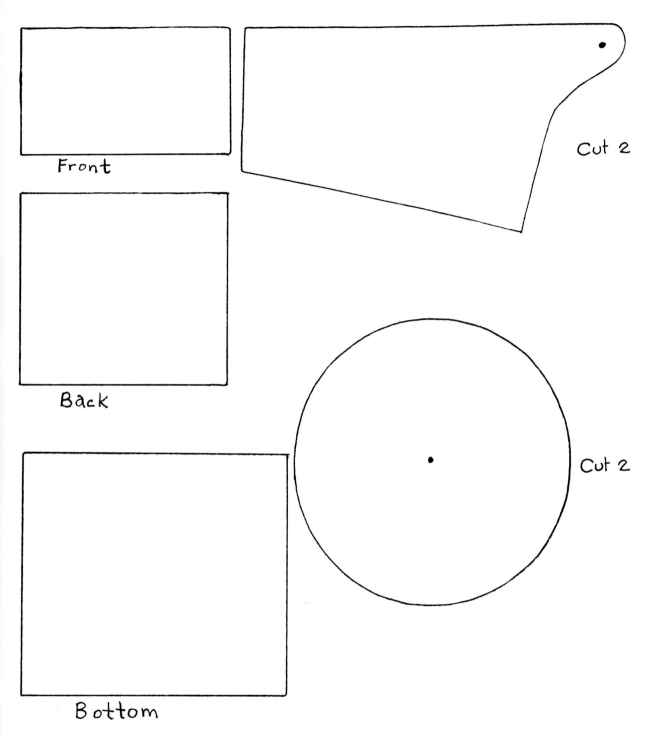

Front

Cut 2

Back

Bottom

Cut 2

Illus. 99. Wheel and cart patterns.

the rabbit onto ¾-in. wood. Trace the legs and arms onto ⅜-in. wood, and then trace wheel, cart, and ear patterns onto ¼-in. wood.

Cutting. Use a scroll saw or band saw to cut out the above pieces; then cut a 3-in. length of ⅛-in.-diameter dowel. Also cut two ¾-in. lengths of dowels. These will be used to attach the wheels and form the handle.

Drilling. With a ³⁄₃₂-in. bit, drill holes through the body of the rabbit and through the arms and legs as indicated on the patterns (Illus. 98).

Use the ⅛-in. bit to drill holes through the wheel centers and cart side-sections. Drill a hole through the "hands" of the rabbit using the ³⁄₃₂-in. bit.

Sanding. With either a stationary belt sander or a sanding wheel, sand all pieces (except ears) so that edges are well rounded. Ears are small and best sanded by hand. Give each piece a final hand-sanding with a fine-grade sandpaper.

Gluing. Glue the sides of the cart to the front and back, as shown in Illus. 100. When completely dry, glue bottom in place and set aside to dry.

Note: Ears can also be glued in place (positions are staggered), or you can drill holes through the head and ears and insert a dowel to make the ears moveable.

Painting. Paint the rabbit and cart with the following paint mixtures. Remember that measurements are approximate.
Rabbit: 2 tsp. white / few drops burnt umber
Cart: 1 tsp. red / few drops black
Wheels: ½ tsp. green / few drops black
Eye: dot of white / dot of black

Assembling. Cut 2 lengths of copper wire approximately 2¾ in. long. Using needle-nose pliers, bend one end of each wire into a small, closed loop. Attach the legs and arms with the wires, as shown in Illus. 101, and then bend the other end of the wires into a closed loop also. Tighten the wires against the arms and legs to ensure positioning.

Tap a small ¾-in. section of dowel into each wheel center, and then tap into place

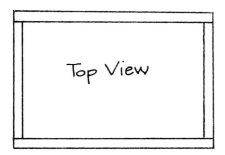

Illus. 100. Gluing sides to front and back.

Illus. 101. Attaching wires to arms and legs.

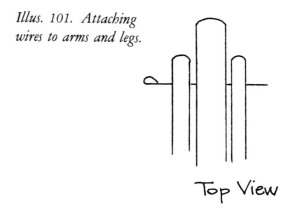

Top View

on the cart. Dowels should protrude about ⅛ in. on the outside of the wheel.

Slide the 3-in. length of dowel into the side of the cart for the handle. Simultaneously, slide the hands of the rabbit onto the handle between the sides of the cart (Illus. 102).

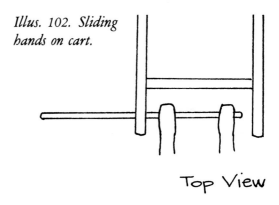

Illus. 102. Sliding hands on cart.

Top View

Gnome with Cart

This charming character can be used as a toy or as a decorative piece of folk art. Fill his cart with candies, miniature presents, or toys.

MATERIALS

Pine, ¾ in. thick: 5 x 6 in.
Pine, ⅜ in. thick: 4 x 8 in.
Birch plywood, ¼ in. thick: 6 x 12 in.
Wooden dowel, ⅛-in. diameter: 6 in.
Copper wire, 14 gauge: 6 in.
Acrylic paint: titanium white, turner's yellow, naphthol red light, permanent green deep, burnt umber, mars black
Wood glue
Sandpaper: medium and fine grades
Tracing paper
Poster board

TOOLS

Scroll saw or band saw
Stationary belt sander or sanding wheel
Drill with ⅜₂-, ⅛-, ⅜₂-in. bits
Needle-nose pliers

INSTRUCTIONS

Pattern. Trace pattern pieces and transfer onto poster board. Cut out poster-board patterns, and then trace wheel and cart pattern pieces onto ¼-in. wood. Trace the gnome body onto ¾-in. wood, and the legs and arms onto ⅜-in. wood.

Cutting. With a scroll saw or band saw, cut out all the above pieces plus a 3-in.

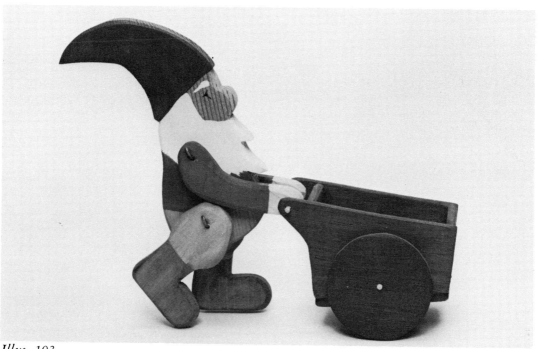

Illus. 103.

114

length of ⅛-in.-diameter dowel. Also cut two ¾-in. lengths of dowel. These will be used to attach the wheels and to form the handle.

Drilling. Drill a hole through the torso, legs and shoulders using the 3⁄32-in. bit. With the ⅛-in. bit, drill the wheel centers and cart sides, as marked on the patterns (Illus. 105). Use the 3⁄32-in. bit to drill holes into the hands. This slightly

larger bit will enable the dowel to slide into the hands more readily.

Sanding. Use either a stationary belt sander or sanding wheel to round the edges of each piece. The rounder the edges on the gnome, the more carved he will appear. Give all pieces a final sanding, by hand, with a fine-grade sandpaper.

Gluing. Glue the sides of the cart to the

Illus. 104. Body patterns for gnome. Pattern at left represents smaller gnome shown on page C of the color section.

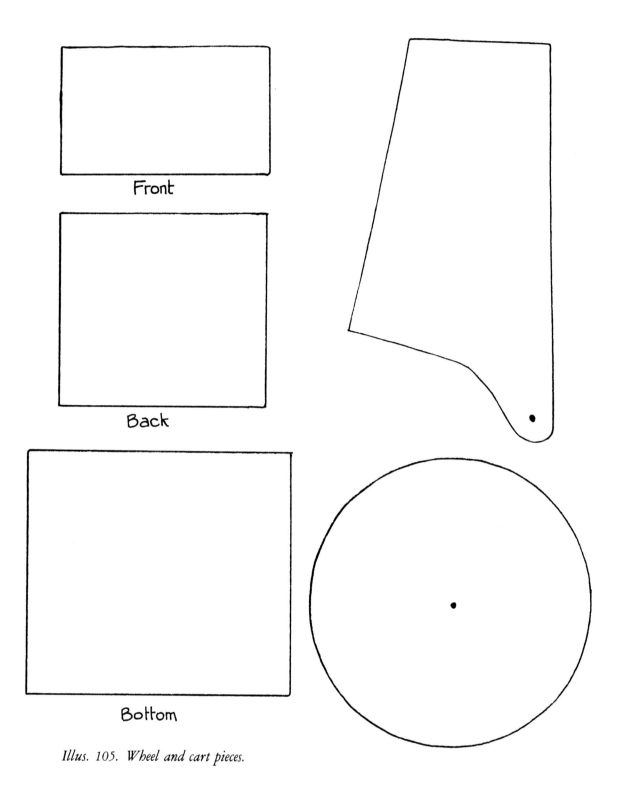

Front

Back

Bottom

Illus. 105. Wheel and cart pieces.

front and back sections. When dry, glue the bottom in place.

Painting. Paint the gnome and cart using the following mixtures of paint. Remember that measurements are approximate.
Cart, hat, jacket: 2 tsp. red / few drops of black
Wheels: ½ tsp. green / few drops of black
Pants: ½ tsp. yellow / drop of burnt umber
Beard, eyebrows: ½ tsp. white / drop of burnt umber
Boots: watered-down burnt umber

Assembling. Cut two 2¾-in. lengths of copper wire. Using needle-nose pliers, bend one end of each wire into a small, closed loop. Attach the legs and arms with the wires, as shown in Illus. 107, and then bend the other ends of the wires into small, closed loops also. Tighten the wires against the arms and legs to ensure good positioning.

Tap a small ¾-in. section of dowel into the center of each wheel, and then tap dowel into place on the cart. Dowels should protrude about ⅛ in. on the outside of the wheels.

Slide the 3-in. length of dowel into the side of the cart for the handle. Simultaneously, slide the hands of the gnome onto the dowel, and then push the dowel through the other side of the cart, with an equal distance of the handle extending on either side of the cart (Illus. 108).

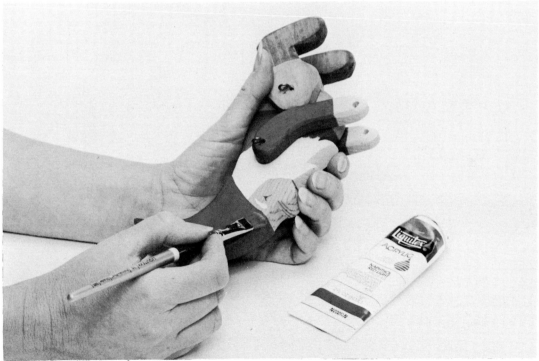

Illus. 106. Painting the gnome.

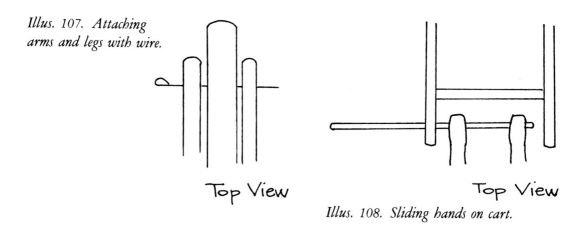

Illus. 107. Attaching arms and legs with wire.

Top View

Top View

Illus. 108. Sliding hands on cart.

Acrobats

These two whimsical acrobats will provide hours of fun and amusement as they perform their many antics and daring feats on the high bar.

Monkey

MATERIALS
Pine, ¾ in. thick: 6 x 7 in.
Birch plywood, ¼ in. thick: 3 x 4 in.
Wooden dowel, ⅛-in. diameter: 6½-in. length

Illus. 109.

Wooden dowel, ½-in. diameter: two ½-in. lengths
Wooden drawer pulls, 1-in. diameter: two
Copper wire, 14 gauge: 4 in.
Wood glue
Acrylic paint: titanium white, mars black, cerulean blue hue, red oxide, burnt umber
Sandpaper: medium and fine grades
Tracing paper
Poster board

Wooden dowel, ⅝-in. diameter: two ⅝-in. lengths
Wooden finials, ¾-in. diameter: two
Copper wire, 14 gauge: 4 in.
Wood glue
Acrylic paint: turner's yellow, hooker's green, naphthol red light, titanium white, mars black, burnt umber
Sandpaper: medium and fine grades
Tracing paper
Poster board

Jester

MATERIALS
Pine, ¾ in thick: 6 x 7 in.
Birch plywood, ¼ in. thick: 4 x 4 in.
Wooden dowel, ⅛-in. diameter: 5½-in. length

TOOLS
Scroll saw or band saw
Stationary belt sander or sanding wheel
Drill with 3/32-, ⅛-, 5/32-in. bits
Needle-nose pliers

INSTRUCTIONS

Pattern. Trace patterns and transfer onto

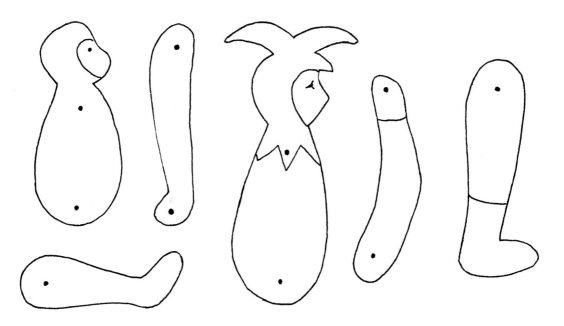

Illus. 110. Patterns for monkey and jester.

poster board. Cut out poster-board patterns, and then trace either the monkey or jester onto the ¼-in. wood. Before cutting these pieces out, draw lines for the following base pieces onto ¾-in. wood.

JESTER: one 3½ x 3½-in. piece; one 4¼ x 4¼-in. piece; two ¾ x 8-in. pieces

MONKEY: one 3 x 3-in. piece; two ¾ x 7-in. pieces

Cutting. Using a scroll saw or band saw, cut out all the pieces for either the jester acrobat or monkey acrobat. Use extreme caution when cutting out the small pieces. Also cut the lengths of dowel listed in the materials list.

Drilling. With a ⁵⁄₃₂-in. bit, drill holes into the arms, legs, and body of the acrobat. Use a ⅛-in. bit to drill partway into the short dowel pieces, which will be used as caps for the bar. Also drill a ⅛-in. hole into the hands of the acrobats. The hands should fit snugly on the bar.

Next, drill a hole through the bar supports, approximately ¾ in. from the top, using a ⁵⁄₃₂-in. bit.

Sanding. Sand larger pieces with the stationary belt sander, rounding all edges. Sand smaller pieces by hand, and then give each piece a final sanding, by hand, with a fine-grade paper.

Gluing. Glue the base pieces together, as shown in Illus. 109; then set aside to dry.

Painting. The acrobats should be painted with the following mixtures. Remember that measurements are only approximate.

MONKEY
Monkey face, supports: ½ tsp. white / drop of burnt umber
Body: ½ tsp. red oxide
Base, caps: ½ tsp. black
Finials: ⅛ tsp. blue / drop of black / drop of white
Eye: dot of white / dot of black

JESTER
Hat, sleeves, caps: ¼ tsp. yellow / drop of burnt umber
Suit, finials, base: 1 tsp. green (watered-down for jester's suit)
Boots, supports: 1 tsp. red / drop of black
Face, hands: ⅛ tsp. white / drop of red / drop of burnt umber
Draw eye with a pen.

Assembling. For each acrobat, cut two 2-in. pieces of copper wire. Bend one end of each wire, using needle-nose pliers, into a small, closed loop. Attach the arms and legs as shown in Illus. 111, and then bend the remaining straight ends into closed loops.

Illus. 111. Attaching arms and legs with wire.

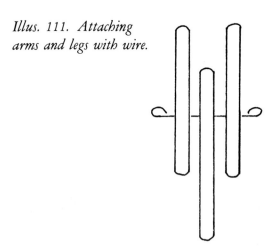

Insert the dowel bar into one support, and then slide the hands onto the bar and into the center, while also sliding the bar through the remaining support. Make sure the hands are centered; if they are so loose that they turn freely around the bar, they will have to be glued in place.

Glue the caps and finials into place. When dry, these acrobats will be ready to perform. Use the caps as handles; turn slow or fast for a variety of comical tricks.

Jumping Jockey

Unique and intriguing, this is a reproduction of an antique balancing toy. Tip the horse and he and his rider will rock back and forth endlessly.

MATERIALS
Pine, ¾ in. thick: 8 x 8 in.
Pine, ⅜ in. thick: 5 x 6 in.
Birch plywood, ¼ in thick: 3 x 3 in.
Wooden drawer pull, 2-in. diameter: one
(or similar round object)

Metal rod, ¹⁄₁₆-in. diameter: 12-in. length
Epoxy glue
Wood glue
Acrylic paint: titanium white, mars black, naphthol red light, burnt umber
Sandpaper: medium and fine grades
Tracing paper
Poster board

TOOLS
Scroll saw or band saw
Stationary belt sander
Drill with ¹⁄₁₆-in. bit

INSTRUCTIONS

Pattern. Trace the pattern pieces and

Illus. 112.

123

Illus. 113. Horse and rider patterns.

Illus. 114. Jump pattern.

transfer onto poster board. Cut out the poster-board patterns, and then trace the horse and rider onto the ⅜-in. wood. Trace the legs and arms onto ¼-in. wood. The jump should be traced onto ¾-in. wood.

Also draw a 3½ x 7½-in. base piece on the ¾-in. wood.

Cutting. Use either a scroll saw or band saw to cut out the pieces for the jumping jockey. Use extra caution while cutting out the small arms and legs.

Drilling. With a ¹⁄₁₆-in. bit, drill into the underside of the horse, as indicated on the pattern (Illus. 113), to a depth of approximately ¾ in. Using the same bit, drill a hole into the center of the wooden ball to approximately the same depth.

Sanding. With a stationary belt sander, carefully sand all edges until rounded. Give each piece a final sanding, by hand, with a fine-grade paper.

Gluing. Glue the arms and legs of the jockey in place. Then glue the jump to the base and set aside to dry.

Painting. Use the following mixtures to paint the horse and jockey, remembering that measurements are only approximate.
Horse: ½ tsp. white / drop of burnt umber
Shirt: ⅛ tsp. red / drop of black
Pants: ⅛ tsp. white / ⅛ tsp. black
Hair: drop of red / drop of burnt umber
Hat, boots, ball: ½ tsp. black
Jump, base: 1 tsp. blue / ¼ tsp. white / ⅛ tsp. black.
Eye: dot of white / dot of black

Assembling. Before cutting the 12-in. metal rod to the proper length, you will have to make adjustments if your wooden weight or the thickness of wood differs from the type of weight or thickness of wood given in the materials list. In other words, proceed carefully.

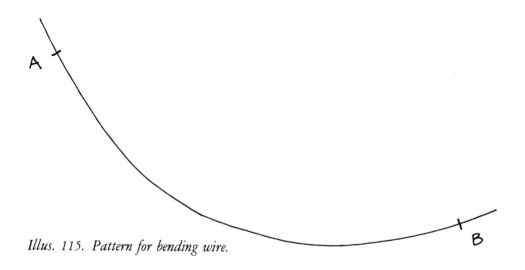

Illus. 115. Pattern for bending wire.

If you suspect that you have some variation, first drill completely through the wooden ball with the $\frac{1}{16}$-in. bit. Next, bend the wire as shown in Illus. 115. Glue end A into the underside of the horse, keeping the wire parallel to the horse. Set this aside to dry thoroughly.

Slide the wooden ball onto the other end of the wire and move it up to point B. Set the horse in the middle of the jump and test the balance. The horse should rock back and forth freely. If balance is off, move the ball up and down the wire at $\frac{1}{16}$-in. intervals until you find the balance point.

Once you have properly balanced the toy, cut off the excess wire, and then glue the wire into the ball.

The wire for the original toy is cut to $6\frac{1}{2}$ in.; however, to avoid any problems, check the balance before cutting the wire.

INDEX